D0981698

ASCENSION!

An Analysis of the Art of Ascension as Taught by the Ishayas

by

MSI

Printed and bound in the United States of America.
Second Printing
SFA Publications
23632 Highway 99 #F-196
Edmonds, WA 98026

ISBN #0-931783-51-8
Library of Congress Catalog Card Number: 95-061427

To my Teacher,
my students,
and all who dedicate their lives to Truth
this collection of papers is dedicated
with love.

CONTENTS

OVERVIEW:COSMIC PERSPECTIVE

Where does one begin to define the Ishaya tradition? The Ishayas are an ancient Order of monks, one which claims to stem directly from the Apostle John, following the direct orders of Christ to preserve his teachings until the third millennium. They hold that the original teachings of Jesus were not a belief system at all, but rather a mechanical series of techniques to transform human life into a constant perception and knowing of the perfection of divinity within every human heart.

What is the source or goal of human life? The mind in the waking state is filled with opposing thoughts. Is the perfection of life to be found after death? Is Heaven a far-off state, one to be attained by living a "good" life, or is it something that is at hand -- a reality that can be attained here and now, an Ascended reality that is possible to be achieved in the present?

Is it possible to live an ideal, Heavenly life in this world? Is it possible to live every moment in an upward-directed, Ascending mode, in which every thought, word and deed is filled with bliss and love and life? Can individual life become ideal? Can it be completely healed of the pain of past loss and faulty belief?

Logically, it is impossible to heal individual life if the world is not healed. No one is isolated from the rest of humanity; all are woven together in a tapestry of energy and synergy in which the lives and actions of one reflect in all others. If one person suffers, all suffer -- at least to some extent. Recognizing this, the ancients formulated a lofty ideal, perhaps best expressed as the Boddhisattva pledge in Buddhism -- "I will not leave this world until all are enlightened." Such commitment is enshrined in these words. Such love. But are they practical?

2 Ascension!

Is it even possible to heal the Earth? If everyone in the entire world must be healed for our individual lives to be ideal, how could it ever happen? Is this not clearly an impossible task for any one being to accomplish? And yet if we desire the impossible, do we desire alone? Many of our greatest throughout history have spoken of a New World, a coming time in which all the problems of life have been solved or Ascended, in which all of humanity unites in seeking the highest and best for everyone. Lofty visions? Surely, but are they also practical? Can they be attained? Or were our spiritual leaders and visionaries speaking only to inspire us to be better?

Do we any longer have a choice? Perhaps it seemed that we did before our modern times, perhaps in previous ages we could delegate some few of us to focus on healing everyone through religion or mysticism or science, but no longer. Even a cursory look at the state of the world leads to the inescapable conclusion that we no longer have a choice. Heal the world we must, else it and we fail to survive. We as a species have created an imbalance on Earth that could in the space of a few days or hours result in the end of our race or the end of our world or both. Is there hope for us? Do we have allies in this healing process? Do the Laws of Nature favor our healing or our elimination? Let's look at the nature of the world and see if there is any hope.

The world is always changing. The Universe is in a constant state of flux. It may have periods of greater or lesser stability, or areas where change seems slight or rare, but these are only temporary realities. The mightiest mountains are worn down to foothills; the oceans rise up and turn into dry land; even the continents slip around on the Earth's molten core like ice on a hot tin stove. One day the Sun itself will die; eventually this galaxy will be extinct, filled with the hollow memories of burned out stars.

The dinosaurs ruled the Earth for a great many more million years than the present human race is supposed to have existed, but where are they now? Life *is* change.

Our world is changing, and ever more rapidly. There are those who take this as evidence that this is not an ideal world, it was not created by perfection or it is not maintained in perfection. This conclusion seems rock solid. But is it? Is this not saying that there is a part of space or time where the Infinite Perfection of the Ascendant is not found? If that is so, then the Infinite is not Omnipresent, or is opposed by a nearly Omnipotent destructive power that seeks to undermine the intent of Infinity. Or perhaps it is all truly random, there is no underlying order; all thought of Ascendant harmony is a myth, created by hopeful people with little common sense.

This kind of thinking denies both logic and experience, as will become clear as we proceed with this short text. There is another way to view this world; there is another way to view all of life.

Change *appears* to be either constructive or destructive. There *seem* to be two great natural forces at work in our Universe -- evolution and devolution. But on closer examination, every motion of devolution is not without purpose, for it opens the pathway for more and greater evolution. It is only when the bud is destroyed that the flower can emerge. It is only when the child dies that the adult is born.

The combined working of these two infinitely opposed forces is all-powerful in the relative cosmos, and is certainly brilliantly wise. Some have considered it mindless, but even a cursory look at the magnificent complexity of any aspect of our Universe makes such a conclusion seem extremely naive. A thousand billion galaxies each with an average of two hundred billion stars? Fifty trillion cells in every human body all working together in perfect harmony? Such wisdom there is in Nature, such brilliance. Natural laws certainly seem all-powerful and all-knowing from our human perspective, do they not?

So, if there are Omnipotent and Omniscient forces at work in our Universe, why do they so often handle our lives in such a destructive manner? Aren't we often crushed by oppressive weights beyond our ability to control? Which of us has not from time to time thought our lives are about as important to the higher powers of Nature as are the insects on our windshields? The universal forces don't seem to have much regard for the little human lives on our planet, do they?

Appearance is a wonderful magician, an extraordinary deceiver, capable of convincing our hearts and minds of the strangest lies. How often do we choose our clothes, houses, jobs by the most superficial standards? And our friends and mates as well. Is this bad? Not necessarily. Compromising integrity doesn't make a whole lot of difference if there is no absolute standard. If we have never seen the Sun, choosing between which star we wish to guide us is not so important. This doesn't mean we might not believe it important and fight with all our might to defend the supremacy of our individually chosen star. We might go to war defending the importance of Sirius, the brightest; we might say that any who refuse to follow the sure council of Polaris, the steadiest, are doomed to hell and Infinite torture; we might create entire philosophies on the, wondrous counsel offered by the most glorious constellation, Orion -- but what happens to our beliefs and philosophies based on starlight when the Sun rises?

The point is that if we attempt to apply the standards of sensual perception in an attempt to understand our position and role in the Universe, we will necessarily fall far short of learning anything of much importance. How to align our understanding with the Cosmic and Universal Forces instead of with the gross material world reported to us by our senses is the whole purpose of inner growth.

Cosmic Intelligence is one name for that Force which pushes our individual lives and our world toward perfection. It is the Source of the harmony between the opposing natural laws that causes all of life to progress, in spite of the appearances on the surface. According to the Ishayas, our only responsibility here on Earth is to make sure that we are not working against Cosmic Intelligence, either consciously or unconsciously.

Evolution on Earth is accelerating at an ever-increasing rate. The vibratory rate of our world is changing upward so quickly now that there is a real danger large numbers will fail to make this transition. It is our obligation to do whatever we can to enable as many as possible to negotiate this global shift in awareness successfully. This should not be considered a burden; it is a joyous movement upward into the light; every step forward on this path is not only great good fortune for every individual but a large upsurge in life for the world's billions.

We have a little time left, a decade or two for most of us, before this transition will be complete. It is time for all the co-workers for peace, all those who wish to be or already are enlightened, all those who possess goodwill for humanity, all leaders everywhere to drop their surface and petty differences and unite with one voice of understanding and praise for the Source of all that is. The simple guiding principle here is this: if we are sowing division, preaching destruction, seeking or finding evil in the world (even if we are looking for it with the intention of removing it!), then we are part of the problem, not the cure.

It may seem possible for a short time longer to oppose the great transformation that is rapidly building in this world. But this is appearance merely. And even that appearance is necessarily going to change. Those who desire to oppose Cosmic Intelligence will soon -- very soon -- be no longer found on this Earth. Everyone will either consciously or unconsciously act in perfect harmony with Universal Mind. Those who would oppose it will either change or simply cease to be here. That is our future. And the good news is that anyone's inner realization helps change the destiny of everyone else.

Some of us have already remembered that we are multi-dimensional beings. We, living on the Earth, are opened to Universal Mind. The Voice of the Universe speaks through us. Desire to serve our fellow wanderers is the natural byproduct of our enlightenment: our perennial task is to help everyone discover Universal Mind within. But words are limited, finite tools; our proper subject is the Unlimited, the Infinite, a subject that lies forever far beyond the ability of language to describe or communicate. Writing or reading or listening to lectures does not expand consciousness; this happens only through direct, personal experience. Hence, is this book short. But the invitation is long.

Security, peace, happiness, health and love await those who learn the Ishayas' Ascension techniques. You may already have recognized in your heart that this offer is for you. But it may take some more time, or perhaps some further exchange of energy or knowledge between us, before your conscious mind understands your heart's choice. This little book is for you; it is designed to help your rational mind learn what your heart already knows full well. Take what you will from this storehouse, drink as deeply as you care from the wellsprings here, and then if we are not to meet again, go your own way with the blessings of this knowledge upon your heart.

The urgency of action now to fulfill our collective destiny is the theme of this work. The world must rise to a state of all-time peace and soon, else many suffer and die needlessly. Answered within this text are many of the fundamental mysteries of life; this is true for any willing to examine this book with an open mind and an innocent heart. As these awaken to the innermost Reality of their wonderful, exalted souls, the trends of life for all beings on the Earth will be irrevocably changed.

This is a precious knowledge, a priceless gift to share with the world.

We are attempting to communicate with you for a specific purpose. There are many who entered here when we did to be with us; if you are among their number, now is the time to come forward and begin to move together with us to our common goal for the good of all.

Take the time to seek out the Ishayas and learn for yourself these mechanical techniques to transform life. Belief is not required -- all that is necessary is that you have an open mind and heart and are willing to give these techniques a chance. If you do this simple thing, I promise you: your life will unfold and blossom in ways you never dreamed possible. There will remain no compromise in you, no living a half or partial life, only the freedom of expanding love and joy in the perfection of fully enlightened consciousness.

-- *MSI,*
dedicated on Guru Purnimah, 1995

I. SOLVING THE PROBLEMS OF THE WORLD

To change your world, change yourself.

To help this world be a better place must certainly be every thinking human's desire. Our planet is faced with innumerable problems, physical and spiritual; the attempts of our leaders to solve them seem neither wholly pathetic nor wholly laudable. They are doing the best they can; even the apparent exceptions to this rule act positively, given the definitions of reality to which they ascribe. But, as courageous as the noble attempts to solve Earth's problems have always been, and as successful as some of the solutions have proved to be in some limited areas of concern, still the over-all depth, breadth and intensity of the difficulties facing the world have only increased over the centuries until the existence of the biosphere and of humanity itself is today swinging in the balance.

It was disastrous for the Carthaginians when the Romans burned Carthage to the ground; it was certainly unfortunate for the Israelites when Rome razed Jerusalem and sent her people into captivity; it was devastating to the Native Americans when the Europeans moved westward; but today we seem determined to destroy the entire world.

It was tragic when the Sahara swallowed the fertile fields of Africa due to human incompetence, but today we lose a football size field of rain forest *every second*; every year, an area of rain forest the size of Pennsylvania is burned and converted to pasture, losing forever not only the wondrous potential pharmaceuticals growing there in their natural state but simultaneously cutting the throat of the largest oxygen-producing organism in the world.

We have all enjoyed the benefits of aerosols and cars

and air conditioners, but the ozone deteriorates. It seems that soon being outside anywhere at any time of day will be deadly.

It was a great accomplishment when our miracle drugs dramatically reduced infant deaths, but today we have well over three hundred million people eking out lives of barest subsistence without meeting the needs of minimal nutrition. Three hundred million of our fellow humans are malnourished or starving today. What did you have for dinner?

Any solution designed to solve any of these problems or the myriad of others facing humanity is certainly good and should be encouraged. But it is not now and will never be sufficient to address the problems of the human condition one at a time, or even in groups of related problems at one time. We can link acid rain, ozone depletion, the ruining of our rivers, lakes and seas with excesses in our technologies, but the basic issue will remain untouched by any such approach. The reason for this is simple. We can attempt to solve a vast number of problems, but the solutions will always cause more problems *as long as we do not know the result of our actions*. With limited minds, obstacles will continue to mutate and evolve as do bacteria in response to our latest miracle drug. A host of new and worse difficulties will continue to arise until the day we change the fundamental error of our thinking.

There is a field next to this house where I'm writing these words. A year ago it was a pasture where a dozen horses grazed. Today it holds thirty houses; another fifteen are scheduled for completion within the next six months. From the standpoint of the silent field, this must feel exactly like a cancerous growth. What utility do these houses have in relation to the land? Where once there was a mutual harmony of organic life, now there is concrete, asphalt, chaos, death. And yet the new residents living here are grateful for this relatively cheap housing: for many of these young families, this is their first escape from apartments into the grand experiment of private ownership. And in another thirty years, this will doubtless be a quiet, even a sedate neighborhood, with tall, stately oaks and maples lining the streets.

I remember climbing up a huge old stump -- twice as high as I was tall, four times as wide as it was high -- down the hill from the house where I grew up in Seattle. It was in the middle of a forty acre tract which we called, "The Swamp." This ground was not particularly swampy, at least not much more than anything of Seattle, but calling it The Swamp added a certain dark mystery to young children. Fifty years before I entered The Swamp in awe and wonder, there was a magnificent stand of Western red cedar and Douglas fir there. A hundred years before that, the evergreens were so thick and tall all over Western Washington that anyone magically transported there from today would think they had wandered into the most wonderful park on the Earth. What a tragedy from the perspective of the Native Americans! But our small tragedy when The Swamp was razed and turned into the sterile asphalt of a parking lot and the plastic and steel of a shopping mall was no less tangible and painful for our childish sensibilities. And yet the close proximity of the nascent stores was viewed as a Godsend by several senior citizens of our neighborhood.

I remember looking for an ancestral home with my family when I was nine. We could not find it -- it was gone, a memory now only, replaced by one more freeway off-ramp. This in the middle of a wheat field in Eastern Washington! A serious loss, surely -- but those who use the freeway every day to hurry home to their families might disagree.

What exactly is a problem? A great evil from one perspective may prove a blessing from another. But even if we can find some problems that everyone can agree are definitely problems, it does not follow that everyone will agree on the solutions. And even if everyone everywhere were to agree on the problems *and* the solutions, there is no guarantee that the solutions would work. Even if everyone everywhere agreed beyond the slightest doubt that the Sun circled the Earth, our planet and our neighbor star would not be likely to deviate from their orbits. Reality is not democratic! Regardless of how much we would like everyone to believe in our cherished dream worlds, it doesn't make them real for anyone other than our own selves.

Don't assume I am implying that it is wrong to attempt to solve any and all problems. Everything that can be done should certainly be done. What I am saying is that our solutions have never worked well because we as a species have never addressed the one fundamental problem that is causing all the others. *How do we transform our actions so that they have only life-supporting effects?*

Until this basic issue is addressed, it will never be possible to solve the myriad difficulties of the human condition. How can this be done?

ONE IDEAL PERSON

If we look into diversity, we see only diversity. When we look outward through our eyes, we see an extremely complex and variegated world. Trying to change this outer world is difficult or impossible by addressing any situation, one at a time. That is why corporations succeed -- a hundred individuals can do a great deal more than one alone. Even if that one is far more efficient and talented than any other of the hundred, it is physically impossible for any one person to do a hundred tasks at once.

Thus are hierarchies structured; thus are civilizations created.

The individual employee may have little or no understanding of how his or her part is contributing to the whole; the private citizen may lack any comprehension of the nature or orderliness of his or her society, but this does not inhibit the effectiveness of the whole. How does an organization function smoothly, be it a cow, a company or a country? Each member of the hierarchial structure of the organization must function well. The health of the organization is determined by the health of its individual members. This is a universal law, be our conversation about organs and their constituent cells or civilizations and their constituent citizens. Who can save a heart if its cells are dying? Who can save a country if its citizens are degenerating?

This may all appear much too simplistic, much too obvious, and yet wholly impossible to change. "Of course," you may say, "your point is clear. If we want to solve the world's problems, we must solve the problems of the individual. There is nothing novel there. Confucius in ancient China said much the same thing. 'When the father is a father and the son a son, when the brother is a brother and the sister a sister, when the husband is a husband and the wife a wife, then the family is set in order. When the family is set in order, the village is set in order. When the village is set in order, the nation is set in order. When the nation is set in order, the world is set in order.' This is all too obvious. If I am healthy in my body, my mind and my spirit, then, you imply, my society will be healthy. If I don't contribute to the world's problems, then the world's problems will cease. But what you offer is just too simplistic. Even if I act perfectly, what of my brother George? Or my husband Sam? What about my kids? Or Fred down the street? Or the big corporations? Or the banks and savings and loans? Or the military-industrial complex? Or terrorists? Or whoever else happens to be on my 'bad' list at the moment? They'll still be damaging the world, just as before. Of what value, then, your solution? It is impossible to apply this thinking globally."

Indeed, I must agree with you. The thought of changing everyone on the planet to become ideal, a person who does nothing to damage either himself/herself or the world in any way, even the slightest, is a concept that sounds too difficult to achieve in any reasonable amount of time. Even identifying which of our daily actions are in fact damaging to ourselves or others is a matter for limitless controversy. The simplest choice presented to each of us at most grocery store check-out counters makes the insoluble riddles of antiquity seem like child's play. "Paper or plastic," the clerk asks us sweetly. What do we reply?   Kill a tree or use a non-renewable, non-biodegradable resource? Which do you choose? Does it matter to yourself or to your world? Is it even worth considering, or is it a momentary and essentially pointless diversion?

The root difficulty with the typical waking state of consciousness is that it is impossible to know *anything* with certainty. It is not now nor will it ever be possible to know all the effects of an action -- of any action, even the most basic. So why not live a life of compromise? Everyone sacrifices integrity on the altar of convenience. Why be any different?

This is the issue that has led many of our philosophers to conclude that there is no Absolute standard of morality or action. This dilemma has caused many others never to question but to let other "authority" figures dictate their actions and beliefs. Without an Absolute standard, such leaders may or may not have anything worthwhile to say; but many of them have at least demonstrated a certain skill in convincing others to listen to them!

It may seem impossible to change everyone in the world. *Fortunately, that is not your responsibility.* It is not your responsibility to change your countrymen, not your neighbors, not your friends, not even your own family. You have the responsibility to change just one person in the entire Universe! Do you know who this all-important person is? Do you know who has created and maintains your private Universe? The good news and the terrible news is exactly the same -- it is you. The one controller of your life and fate is you, no one other than you. You have made it exactly as you willed. Perhaps your choices were unconscious until today, perhaps you did not know any better before. But those days are over now. Since you have done it, you can do it over in any way you choose.

There may be others working to help everyone else change, but that need not be your concern. You don't have to see all the plan; you don't have to understand its whole operation. You don't even have to know exactly how your part fits into the whole. It isn't necessary! All you have to do is live your own part perfectly and your world will transform around you. That is guaranteed, absolutely guaranteed. If the light within you is not dark, the shadows will fly from your world.

How impossible a task, saving the world. How possible a task, saving yourself. Cleanse your own heart and the world's heart will be cleansed.

The waking state perception of the Universe is completely reversed, upside-down. In the waking state, we commonly think that our effect is greater when we act outwardly; we think that our actions are stronger than our words and our words are stronger than our thoughts. Therefore, for example, we do not speak our resentment but hold it inside, festering, until it erupts in attacks far greater than the original action we did not take, or until it kills us. This way of living is backwards, it is destructive, it cures nothing and complicates everything.

One human's thoughts can change a world. To be healed, the world does need one Ideal Person. This person has already been born, this person has a name and a personal history. The birthdate of this person is yours, the personal history is yours, this person's name is yours. This Ideal Person is you.

We affect more than we can possibly know. With every mood, every thought, every word, every gesture, we change our lives and our Universe.

II. CHANGING LIFE

A journey of a thousand miles begins with a single step.

Our vision and understanding of the human condition is cultured by our experience. In the waking state of consciousness, we think we are isolated in space and time from one another; we think we are separate and alone. Because this is our perception and belief, we conclude that it is difficult or impossible to influence others' thinking or behavior deeply. We believe that it is only with great expenditures of energy, time and commitment we can succeed in changing others.

This belief results from the daily experience of our senses. But our senses deceive us, here as everywhere. The reality of our being is that we can, absolutely effortlessly, change not only ourselves but also everyone else on the planet, past, future or present. If this idea appears strange, it is only because we are accustomed to thinking of ourselves as linear and finite beings with strictly circumscribed abilities and functions.

If we think of great-souled members of our race, we often think their actions *are* their accomplishments. But their true accomplishments are the inner Realities they have developed; their outer actions are their raiment merely. The material may be very fine, the pattern exquisitely beautiful, the colors deep and clear, but any cloth is utterly without value compared to the priceless body wearing it.

The race evolves as the collective consciousness of the race evolves. The beliefs of the human race are like the "bell" curve so common in mathematics:

The leading edge of all change begins with a single individual. At first, the fact that the change is happening at all may be unknown to practically everyone, but it grows more and more rapidly with time. From the first person, it spreads naturally to everyone. This process is automatic; if the individual responsible for introducing the change chooses to engage in action to help promote it, this is not required: that would be a generous redundancy.

Our thoughts are not hidden away inside us. We commonly believe they are; we believe (and hope!) some thoughts and beliefs are somehow private, are somehow secret from the rest of the Universe. This is an illusion. Every thought affects everyone and everything everywhere at all times. Because of this, it becomes absurdly easy to change the world: we need only change one person. If I change me, everyone will benefit. The greatest gift you can give those you love is the example of your own life working.

Even if you cannot accept the full range of possibility represented by this concept -- that your improvement improves everyone else -- still there can be no question that you certainly must desire to improve your own life for your own sake. The fortunate truth is that this is not hard to do. In fact, it is extremely easy. Anyone who declared it hard to improve was undoubtedly speaking from his or her own experience -- but that experience must have had as a premise the belief that beneficial change is difficult. The reality of the human condition is that beneficial change is extremely easy, *as long as there is competent guidance.* There is no problem, physical, mental, emotional, or spiritual that cannot be solved effortlessly. The techniques of Ascension are designed to assist in this healing process from the inside out.

We commonly believe that some problems are larger

than others, that some are more difficult or complex than others. But every problem is the same from the standpoint of Infinite Intelligence. They only seem different from the perspective of limited minds. Every problem in life can be solved in exactly the same way -- and that solution is effortless to achieve. It is not now, never has been and never will be difficult to live more of Infinite Intelligence. Rather, it is not now, never has been and never will be difficult to live Infinite Intelligence fully and completely.

The first step toward this goal lies in recognizing the possibility of doing it. If we don't believe something is possible, it will remain impossible for us. Once we realize it is *possible* to be more, the desire to *be* more will naturally take hold of our minds.

The second step lies in acknowledging where we are right now. Most of us are in the habit of denying what we are experiencing *here* and *now*. This is probably because we have judged our present circumstances as being in some way undesirable. Our lives or our environment or the people in our Universe are not viewed as being perfect -- and we typically have a long list of facts that "prove" this set of perceptions and beliefs. "Mary is too fat." "John drinks too much." "Steve is cruel to me and beats me." "I need to be making more money to pay my bills." "My job is OK, but it is not what I really enjoy doing." "Our neighborhood is going downhill." "I am sick." etc.

The lists are endless -- any perception or judgment that someone or something about our world is imperfect is a part of our conclusion that our life is not ideal. Most of us "make the best" of our inadequate and far from perfect world, "doing the best we can" to move ahead in spite of circumstances, even though we didn't marry whom we really wanted or we don't have the job we desired or don't make enough money or we don't live where and how we wish or we are not particularly happy or healthy.

Often our response to our perceived shortcomings is to repress our dissatisfaction. Frequently, we do this to make our lives (or someone else's life) easier. We feel that agreeing with another's opinion is better than cultivating our own.

There was once a beautiful young woman named Leora, who was bright, intelligent, and highly gifted in the arts. She married Sam and had two children. Sam was extremely opinionated about most things. In his case, this was due to an inherent inferiority he experienced around everyone -- he felt others would take advantage of him or try to control him if he didn't strike first. Exposed to Sam's continual and intense opinions, Leora's native intelligence gradually lessened. She began to feel that a "good" wife was one who supported her husband blindly in all things. She became his servant rather than his equal; in all matters, great and small, Leora's voice and reason were an echo of Sam's opinions.

In time, Sam grew bored with Leora's mindless behavior and ran off with another woman who challenged him to think. Leora was crushed and deeply surprised. Hadn't she done everything she could to please him? Desperately longing to be in a relationship -- any relationship! -- she soon found another man, one who to this day treats her exactly the same way Sam did. She could have turned the unfortunate loss of her first husband into an exploration of why her life was as it was. Instead she continued with her fundamental mistake and is still paying the price for it.

This is a frightfully common set of experiences in our modern world. The parent-child relationship is another common version: we, as children, are for years utterly subservient to our parents' will. Our parents are as gods to us;

if they are themselves incomplete individuals, our gods are insane. The effect of this when we enter the adult world is unconsciously to choose to live a life vastly different from the one we would have chosen had we been encouraged to develop our own natural tendencies and talents. We tend to internalize the voices and beliefs of our oppressors: even after the external agent of our subservience is removed by distance or death, we still cower behind their image, unwilling or incapable of being ourselves.

To change, it is helpful to acknowledge where we are right now. This can be an effortless process, a simple intellectual recognition, but for some, so many layers of confusion and delusion about who we are and what we believe stand between us and this recognition. It can take some time -- and patience.

Acknowledgment does not mean simply changing one belief system for another. A common element of the typical "religious conversion" is that our own will is replaced, not by God's will, but by someone's or some group's interpretation of God's will. This is yet another version of the master-slave scenario so common among abusive husbands or wives and abusive parents. This is never conducive to individual freedom or growth. Mental subservience in followers is desired only by incomplete souls, attempting to control their Universe to protect their flawed and fearful view of reality. A true Teacher will always desire his/her students to become self-sufficient -- to master the Teacher's knowledge so that the Teacher is no longer necessary. All True Teachings, then, always point the finger of understanding back at the student's own heart. Only from the inside out can real growth occur.

This process of acknowledgement extends much more deeply into the personality than most individuals have ever consciously gone. One of the most effective ways to do this is through the Ishayas' Ascension. In the process of the Ascension techniques, a specific and highly individualized thought is created by the teacher working with the student as a "vehicle" to "ride" inward to the Source of all thought, the Ascendant.

When an individual Ascends, it becomes unnecessary to try to undo the previous beliefs and judgments; the power of this wholly beneficial inward process is sufficient to remove all previous false perceptions and understandings and replace them with the direct experience of the transcendental beauty and perfection of the Ascendant within. When the inner Reality is thus acknowledged, the outer realities automatically change.

In other words, it is not necessary to *try* to restructure our habits, our beliefs, or any aspect of our minds. It is not necessary ever to berate ourselves for our supposed shortcomings and failures. Once begun, the process of internal transformation and re-organization is completely automatic. A leaf does not have to be taught how to fall to the ground. Once it is removed from its habitual lodging, it falls. The invincible force of Natural Law, gravity, pulls it effortlessly to the ground. The Earth is much larger than the leaf. There is no necessity for the leaf to *try* to fall. Indeed, it would take effort for the leaf *not* to fall! Similarly with the mind. The invincible attractive force of the Ascendant is pulling constantly on our minds. It is requiring excessive use of force to keep from falling inward, into the Ascendant. This is why minds tire so easily; this is why bodies require so much sleep every night. Without a suitable vehicle, how hard it is to move! But if the car is running and full of gas, how simple it is to exert a tiny force on the pedal -- and away we go! Without a suitable vehicle, how hard it is to move into the mind! But with a proper Ascension Technique, how simple it is to choose to Ascend -- and away we go!

Watch yourself closely. What is your response when you think of moving deeper inside? Is it eager anticipation, coupled with an intense desire to learn what is really there? Or is it fear, unreasoning blind terror of the dragons lurking within? Both are common responses to this suggestion. The first is a clear experience of what naturally occurs when we let go, Ascend and grow more fully into life. The second is a clear experience of what naturally occurs when we try to stop ourselves from growing more fully into life.

III. EMOTIONS!

Our birth is but a sleep and a forgetting:
The Soul that rises with us, our life's Star,
Hath had elsewhere its setting,
And cometh from afar;
Not in entire forgetfulness,
And not in utter nakedness,
But trailing clouds of glory do we come
From God who is our home:
Heaven lies about us in our infancy!
Shades of the prison-house begin to close
Upon the growing boy.
But he beholds the light, and whence it flows,
He sees it in his joy;
The Youth, who daily further from the east
Must travel, still is Nature's priest,
And by the vision splendid
Is on his way attended;
At length the Man perceives it die away,
And fade into the light of common day.
As if his whole vocation
Were endless imitation.

-- *Wordsworth,*
Intimations of Immortality

THE ROOT OF STRESS

Our physical bodies came about from the union of a sperm cell produced by our fathers and an egg cell created by our mothers. This made the bodies but not the dwellers in the bodies. More than one ancient system of thinking agrees with Wordsworth: the soul enters human life from Omniscient

Wisdom. If this is so, there is nothing not known to the soul's guardians and to the pre-infant about the lifetime that is being entered; there is nothing not known about the parents, the siblings, the society that awaits. The soul chooses a particular lifetime because it knows that existence will resonate most effectively with its unfulfilled desires and will provide it with all that it needs to move closer to complete realization.

From this perspective, the first problem most or all infants face is that behind the mask of the physical mother and father is the memory of the Divine Mother and Divine Father, the male and female halves of God. As newly returned infants, we identify our biological parents with these flawless Beings: deep inside, we know full well exactly what is and what is not perfection, we know that we desire only love and support from our physical parents and world. We are frustrated and disappointed again and again as our earthly parents fail again and again to match our Eternal Ideal. As an inevitable result, we grow to mistrust our parents and their world. Since most if not all of us are severely deprived of a perfect represen- tation of Divine Love on Earth, we have an emptiness inside that cries to be filled.

This initial disappointment is one of the fundamental foundations of ignorance and one that begins so early and is so subtle it can be extremely difficult to eradicate. Many of us, finding only marginal support from our parents or our environment for our emotions, learned to repress them. A typical young child has no problem expressing his or her feelings. This openness frequently is not acceptable to the adults present because of their own inhibitions; they react with condemnation of the child, with rejection or punishment. Children have no defenses against this. If free and open expression leads to undesirable consequences, there is nothing to do but repress feelings and desires. These attempts to protect the personality result in shutting down innocence and expanded awareness; in time, children become completely lost in their defenses as they create environmentally supported roles.

If we were denied support for our desires as children, we may turn to covert manipulation or outright hostility as the only effective means of fulfilling our wishes. The unfulfilled needs from our childhood continue to manifest in our adult relationships: lacking the ability to communicate our desires clearly, we nevertheless still carry around a host of unfulfilled longings from the past. Do we ask for something as if we expect not to get it? Do we resort to anger or manipulation to fulfill our desires? Do we pout and throw temper tantrums or become cruel if we don't get our way? Do we wait until someone becomes close to us to reveal our hidden agenda? These are obviously not the most effective ways to achieve our ends and yet they are among the most common ways attempted.

Many adults are firmly locked away from true intimacy. The attempt to fill this emotional vacuum can lead to addictive or compulsive behavior patterns -- drugs, alcohol, tobacco, food, illness -- to relationships -- negative or positive -- or, ideally, to the growth of consciousness.

Many adults' sense of self-worth is lacking or damaged in some way. One way we try to maintain the mirage of our self-worth is by criticizing others before they can see what is wrong in us. Or, since in the waking state self-worth is defined almost entirely in terms of the response from the environment, we rely on others to define our lives. This is like putting a band-aid on a festering ulcer; this never leads to lasting happiness or health. Compromising ourselves to be loved and lovable never has and never will make us more worthwhile; continued for a long enough time, this behavior pattern is certain to generate resentment and hostility. The more we deny our own individuality, the more our own power is lost.

Another example of inappropriate expression of feelings is what many consider compassion: if someone is suffering or unhappy, we think that compassion says we should join him/her in his/her misery. This is not compassion, this is not truly loving or caring. Instead of having one lying on the floor crying, now there are two. Responding to another's suffering as if it were our own is not empathy! It is only expressive of our own limitations of spirit. Taking on another's feelings as if they were our own is not compassion! This is not the doorway to intimacy and is doomed to failure, for this is not the path of growth. True compassion means raising the level of consciousness of the sufferer by recognizing that the suffering is misplaced, that it is an impossible event in enlightenment, and then by sharing this vision. This is not done in a condescending or superior manner! This is done with perfect love.

The blockage of true feelings is quite deep and strong in many adults. The left hemisphere-controlled ego-mind of the waking state has learned to judge feelings as uncom- fortable, something to be repressed, controlled, tightly channelled. Of course, since the human personality is extraordinarily flexible, that which is forced down in one area manifests in another. Feelings can never be destroyed. They can only be acknowledged, expressed, lovingly re-channeled, or repressed. Fully living in the present means that no feelings are ever repressed or desires perverted; all are accepted, expressed and fulfilled.

Releasing our blocked and buried feelings is one of the most important aspects of the evolution from the waking state. Unless the destructive behavior patterns and beliefs we absorbed from our parents and our childhood environment are allowed to dissolve, they will continue to warp every area of adult behavior.

The emotional life is like a mighty river, flowing inside us all. When we attempt to dam up a river, the water no longer circulates freely: it stagnates or seeks other means of release. Just as a dam breaking can cause great damage, just so repression of feelings turns our emotions into a destructive, threatening force.

We owe it to ourselves to discover what our feelings and desires really are. It is necessary to stop manipulating ourselves or others to fulfill our needs; honest and open expression alone allows us to channel the power of our emotions positively. Instead of demanding, we must learn to share our true feelings; this enables us not to be a victim of our own uncontrolled defenses and reactions. It is necessary for us to learn to be our own Cosmic Parents: through wisdom and benevolence, we can lovingly recognize and subtly direct our desires without trying to dam them up and struggle with them. This need not be difficult!

As we begin to open the stresses of our past relationships to the light, we naturally begin to recognize the source of our feelings, projections and behaviors. One of the first results is a true forgiveness of our parents' limitations. Blaming them for being incomplete souls is almost as much of a waste of time as is continuing to remain stuck in reactive behavior patterns. Of course they were not Ideal. Who in their world was?

LOVE AND FEAR

There are only two roots to all our emotions: love and fear. Love is the natural state of human life; fear is the means the ego uses to control and possess the world. They cannot simultaneously coexist: When love increases, fear evaporates -- since it was never real, it vanishes in the Sun of perfect love. When fear increases, love hides and bides its time until the individual opens again to Truth. It can never be destroyed, but since the human is endowed with certain inalienable rights (including perfect free will) if the ego insists on illusions, love will as if disappear from the mind until the personality chooses again for Reality.

The ego wants to own everything; this denies the invincibility of surrender, the handmaiden of love. Love is universal and freely given, yet the ego insists that it be owned, that it obey the ego's stern dictates of when, how and where. In this, the ego will forever fail, for it is fighting the wrong battle. Love can never be limited or exist in separation or isolation. Only by renunciation of the desire to manipulate and control will the ego melt into the Universal Self of Infinite, Eternal Love.

It is not by attempting to force feelings to change that they change. Emotions evolve only when they are accepted exactly as they are. The key to doing this is to stop judging them. Only the ego defines good and bad. This is its primary tool of control: if some desires are good and some are not, life is going to remain split. By separating our feelings from the ego's belief systems, we can use their powerful energy for personal growth.

There is a story from the Ishayas that illustrates this point. The monks were attacked from time to time by hordes of demons when they were deep in meditation. No matter how hard they worked to be free from them, there was no escape. It was only when they stopped judging them as evil that they would vanish or transform into celestial nymphs or angels. It was only the monks' interpretation of reality that was giving them trouble. This recognition is a necessary stage of evolution.

As consciousness grows, we learn that whatever comes to us is our own creation, none other's. With the dawn of this understanding, we stop wasting our energy fighting, resenting or repressing what we created. This enables us to use the energy of our desiring to accomplish much faster growth.

THE SHADOW

Inside every human being there is a general division of function between the left and right hemispheres of the brain. The left is more rational, logical, mathematical, scientific. The right is more instinctive, intuitive, emotional, spatial, artistic, creative; this hemisphere is in general more developed in the female of the species. The woman's perspective is therefore typically broader than the man's, for she is more dedicated to nurturing and healing life. What can be repressed in the female is the left hemisphere, the rational, logical and specific ability to focus awareness; in extreme cases, this leads to an argumentative personality that is based in unreasonable thinking, consisting mostly of opinions rather than facts.

The man's typical left hemisphere dominance drives the male to attempt to master Nature. His increased level of dynamism and aggression makes him the preferred member of the relationship to deal with the outer world. In an ideal (enlightened) couple, the female is in charge of the rudder, the man rows the boat: it is typically wiser for the female to be in charge of the over-all direction of the couple's life. What the man may repress is the right hemisphere, for he is uncomfortable with the feminine qualities of instinct and emotion. When developed, the right hemisphere bestows the ability to create, to feel, to love, to experience beauty. In the highest form of balance, the right hemisphere becomes for a man his muse --- his inner guide to complete consciousness.

The repressed portions of ourselves are typically projected onto our partners in relationships. It could be said that there are four beings involved in every relationship: the two we are aware of and the two that are unconscious and are being projected. In the ideal state, these repressed parts, projected outward, lead to the development of the wholeness we lack inside. But when this process is blocked through damaging habits, this projection leads to a continuing series of destructive relationships, for we don't realize we are simply projecting outward our own limitations and stress.

Whenever we find ourselves blaming anyone on the outside for anything, it is always because we have failed to realize that our feelings of depression and incompleteness are coming from the inside. Attempting to condemn anyone on the outside *always* comes because of our own lack of self-esteem and power; we feel helpless and worthless on the inside and project this outside. If this remains unrecognized, no relationship can withstand this destructive power.

When we were children, many of us saw no solution to the conflicting demands of our environment other than hiding away aspects of ourselves. This hidden and repressed shadow inside never matured, but contains numerous fragments of our personality that long for conscious recognition and approval. Since we have intensely judged so much that our personal shadow contains, however, we typically would rather eat nails than look at what is locked away inside us. Like the mummy in the crypt, we'd just as soon it would stay hidden and buried forever. But our shadow contains many beautiful and worthwhile characteristics that never developed because there was no recognition of them in our environment. If in our childhood there was no support for or embodied example of our natural tendencies and latent capacities, we automatically repressed a large and often the better portion of ourselves. This is why celestial perception is so rare in adults, for example. Many children see the elementals, celestials, angels and devas, but the adults in their world laugh at them if they mention their visions; in time the ability to See is shrouded.

Since the shadow represents those parts of ourselves that are repressed, its most common appearance is in projection onto others. The elements in others that we envy or hate are those parts of ourselves that we have judged inappropriate in our current Universe.

The shadow can never be fully repressed or forcibly removed. The only road to resolution is to cease judging. The evolving soul must eventually embrace all the hidden desires, needs and feelings within. Until this happens, the larger part of our energy will remain locked in conflicting subpersonalities that embody our repressed shadow. Until this happens, life continues in imbalance, which can be severe. Facing the personal inner darkness takes courage and humility. A touch of faith is also useful: if we believe that we can start opening the locked inner doorways without damaging ourselves, we can start reintegrating our sundered personalities and stop projecting our judgments and desires onto others.

Without the natural mechanics of evolution through Ascension, this can be painful: for some of us, it takes the shock of seeing ourselves as we really are, instead of how we wish or assume we are, that begins our journey toward enlightenment. But whatever it takes, this recognition is required to culture true freedom. So the only appropriate response becomes not whether or not I have to begin but how quickly can I begin. A journey of a thousand miles begins with a single step. The journey must be taken, lest our shadows continue to warp and kill us; the time to begin is NOW.

Fortunately, through the practice of Ascension, all the repressed areas of the personality are effortlessly, harmoniously and gracefully exposed to the Infinite Light of perfect understanding. This turns what otherwise can be a slow and difficult process into an exciting discovery of increasing joy.

IV. IGNORANCE

What you put your attention on grows.

The waking state of consciousness is often called ignorance, for in this state the Omnipresent Reality of the Infinite Ascendant is not experienced, it is ignored. It is also known as identification: the mind is caught by its interpretations of past experience and is not free to experience the freedom of life as it is in the present moment. It is caught by identification with the boundaries: only the crudest level of objects is perceived; the Unbounded Ascendant is missed. There is no awareness or at best a dim awareness of the Ascendant in the waking state; therefore individual life is caught by identification with desires, thoughts and possessions. This is like losing a million dollars by finding a dime.

The waking state mind is chaotic, incoherent: it is fragmented between thoughts produced by the rational left hemisphere and those created by the true and false emotions of love and fear. Silence and clarity are rare occurrences: the mind is always active, racing from one thought stream to another, from one regret, worry, difficulty, desire or frantic scheme to another. The waking state mind is buffeted like a small boat on a tumultuous sea as its 50,000 thoughts run through daily, almost beyond control.

How do we return to our heritage of Infinite Awareness? How do we attain permanent silence inside? How do we gain true freedom?

To escape from ignorance requires: **(1.)** the **humility** to recognize that many or even all of our cherished waking state beliefs may simply not be true; **(2.)** the **desire** to change; **(3.)** the **courage** necessary to challenge and erase those beliefs that no longer serve us; **(4.) surrender** to Cosmic Will; and **(5.) discipline** (the willingness to adopt relative boundaries to gain Eternal Freedom).

Also required is **(6.) consistency**, or the intelligence to make a choice and then stick with it. Nature does not support vacillation. More accurately, Nature does try to support all human desires, but when these desires are mutually contradictory, what can She do? It takes a consistent choice -- then and then only can the forces of natural law be marshalled to create success.

Abundance in any area of human concern is the result of **(7.) one-pointed commitment.** It does not work to say, "I will change as soon as the external conditions make it possible to change." The Universe can and will out-wait any such ego proposal. What does work is to say, "I will change Now, today; as I move consistently toward my goal, I assume that the means will manifest for me." And of course they do, for instead of resisting the flow of life, the individuality has now aligned with Cosmic Will.

My Teacher commonly said, "The means gather around sattva." Sattva means purity and clarity. Thus **(8.) purity** of life and **(9.) clarity** of intention bring fulfillment in their wake as inevitably as rain from cumulonimbus.

Trying to gain enlightenment without the above necessary qualities of focus is comparable to the attempt of trying to churn butter from water. It will simply never happen. But with Ascension, the wisdom needed to tread the path to enlightenment naturally develops on the basis of increasing charm of experience. Individual life starts changing more and more quickly as the stress in the nervous system decreases; all the requisite conditions for growth are met as the various parts of our personality start cooperating with us. This process is natural and effortless and results in dramatic transformation of every area of human concern.

DEATH OF THE EGO

When we are born, our first requirement is to relate to the outer world. Our need for physical and emotional support means that we must direct our senses outward, away from inner silence and complete consciousness, into the field of multiplicity. In order to do this, we organize our consciousness into an illusory structure that artificially maintains our separation from the inner Ascendant Self. This structure is known as the ego. This was designed as a necessary but temporary stage of development, not the be all and end all of human evolution. The dominance of the ego is not supposed to continue past puberty.

It is our attachment to the ego that keeps us trapped in the world of illusion, in that which is known in Sanskrit as *samsara*. Samsara means literally, "perpetual succession" or "eternal cycle": we rise up only to fall again, over and over again forever until the endless circle is Ascended. Since the ego structure *is* an illusion, everyone on the deepest level inside desires to Ascend this artificial construct. The illusion must be abandoned; the ego must die.

If not properly understood, this process of expansion beyond the confines of the ego can be quite painful. Never having received the critically necessary knowledge, some decide at this point to abandon their quest for enlightenment.

In extreme cases, the intense feeling of emptiness as the old behavior patterns fall away can lead to the desire to die. These suicidal impulses are signs from our higher Self that the old attitudes standing in our way must end. Mastering this process can be an act of purest courage. Without Ascension, the renunciation of the sense-oriented life of the lower self can be horrifying to the ego; the subsequent birth to enlightenment is inconceivable and impossible from the perspective of the illusory structure of mind-created boundaries that is the ego.

A second twisting of the growth of consciousness as the

ego thrashes about in its death throes can occur in life-threatening illness. This challenge can be much more subtle than an overt act of self-destruction, but the cause is the same. The internal spiritual forces are powerful; like the mythical gods of ancient cultures, they can seem temperamental or capricious. If they are ignored or dishonored, they may actively seek to destroy us. Their purpose is of course not to kill us, but to break our addiction to our limited world-views. Through death's dark door, we enter mental states identical to those we discover inside during Ascension. Debilitating illness can have the same effect: like the phoenix from the ashes, an entirely new personality emerges from the painful death of the old.

Ancient shamanic experience echoes this theme: it is only when the initiate accepts the communication from the inner world that the torturing spirit returns him/her to life or health and the new life-role of the shaman begins. The whole purpose of such an event is to dissolve the rigid boundaries of ego-based thinking. Fortunate are those who can accomplish this through Ascension without having to die or experience life-threatening disease!

What is required for our growth is surrender to higher power. Only through this death of our old ego-based thinking does rebirth occur. Becoming immortal through dying is the theme of many ancient myths. Beneath the chaos of the waking state mind lies the perfect silence and beauty of the Infinite bliss of the Ascendant. When the ego is cut away, enlightenment automatically dawns. This is the transfiguration of the ego.

This was symbolically attempted by the death initiation in many ancient (and current aboriginal) cultures. In Egypt, for example, the novitiate priest was instructed to stay inside a sarcophagus until the ego was killed. This process did kill the aspirant on occasion, but when it did not, the priest returned beyond the portals of death with true knowledge from the Ascendant.

In the West, we have the example of the passion of

Christ on the cross as a perfect representation of the requirement of the death of the ego as the doorway to the Ascendant. The crucifying cross represents the opposites of Earth-life, unified at their center, in the Ascendant. The personal self is crucified to give rise to the transcendental Reality of the Son of God.

Until this ultimate transfiguration occurs, we continue to identify with the ego as it represses large parts of our personality in favor of those segmented beliefs which are favored. When we begin to grow in enlightenment, these repressed areas start clamoring for recognition and acceptance; this can lead to intense inner conflict. The opposing forces in our lives rise in strength and power until the death of the world seems imminent. We manifest in our individual lives the ancient mythic battle between two nearly Omnipotent armies facing each other to vie for mastery of the Earth.

And yet it is only through the reconciliation of opposing internal values that full development of consciousness can occur. Universal love is required for us to manifest the all-inclusive nature of the inner Divine Self: love toward all the disparate and hitherto denied portions of ourselves naturally translates into love for everyone and everything in the world. This unconditional love and acceptance is the opposite of judgment, which is *always* based in projection by the fear-based ego.

The ultimate Ascension is when we recognize that all the limited conditions of our belief system must be surrendered to the Omniscient and Omnipotent power of the Ascendant. This results in a radical transformation of our previous ego-structured existence; the small and limited self rises into the Universal. Christ's death and Ascension thus serve as a model for any aspirant to enlightenment. The temporal and the personal are Ascended as universality dawns; the ego melts into the Universal Self.

This is the essence of renunciation, not living the life of the monk or the nun. True renunciation means that all belief in the ego has been given up, not that we deny certain desires or behavior patterns. It is a misinterpretation of the path to enlightenment to feel that it is only suitable for recluses. This comes from a limited and incorrect understanding of the teachings of such enlightened leaders as Christ, Shankara and Buddha.

For example, the Mahayana Buddhists define the three requirements for evolution past the waking state: 1) clear experience of the Ascendant, 2) compassion and 3) renunciation. What was originally meant was the renunciation of thought-bound ego-identity; but what it in time came to be thought to mean was becoming a monk or nun and living the life of a recluse. True renunciation is the natural by-product of clear experience of the Ascendant and has nothing to do with external patterns of living. And similarly with compassion. This is the three-in-one nature of the Ascendant: the mind, the heart and the body all rise to fulfillment together. The knower, the known and the process of knowing all grow in perfection simultaneously.

As change accelerates because of regular Ascension, the ride either becomes much smoother or much rougher. What causes the difference? The regular experience of Reality caused by Ascending shakes all the former beliefs about life. All the old habits and addictions surface for review. Any area of life where integrity has been compromised comes clearly into focus, allowing us to choose again whether or not we wish to continue with the old behavior patterns -- or adopt new ones, based on our changing experience of life.

There are no "do's and don'ts" in Ascension -- none are required or desirable. With regular experience of the underlying Truth, anything that does not serve drops away naturally and inevitably. Even though this is true, there is a transition zone. Are we willing to embrace the changes of Evolution? Or do we resist and attempt to hold onto the past? Attempting to hold on results in pain. It is like trying to squeeze into a suit that is three sizes too small. It hurts.

The river of life pulls us ahead ever more swiftly. If we resist and attempt to hold onto the shore, we get cut and bruised and torn by the rigid boundaries of the land. If we let go and flow, on the other hand, we swiftly flow ahead into a bold new future of adventure and discovery. It is a simple choice, really, and one that can be consciously made at any time. Regardless how strong the tendency to grasp onto things or beliefs, nothing can long resist the wholly beneficial power of correctly practiced Ascension.

Life is joy. The purpose of human life is to expand love. Love heals: there is no infirmity of body, mind, heart or soul that can withstand unconditional love. A loving heart finds joy in every moment. Nothing can resist its power for growth. All the problems in human life come when we attempt to resist the lessons of love. If we attempt to hold onto the past, we suffer and life becomes more complex. If we learn to let go and trust in every moment, in every life situation, we fly ahead on eagle wings into the heart of God, which is pure bliss and Infinite love.

How does one master the transition? By being willing to let go of *everything*. Anything that is real will remain, but the attachment will be gone. It is attachment that binds and causes pain. Freedom from attachment is joy and leads to the fastest and most comfortable growth. Attachment leads to hell.

Does this mean that possessions or relationships are in some way bad? Not at all. The royal family in the palace can be fully enlightened; the hermit in his cave can be much more ignorant -- it is not the possessions themselves which bind, which cause trouble or pain, it is the attachment to them that leads to all problems. To be free, then, be willing to give up *everything* if that is what is required of you. Then your life can become a significant tool for evolution. But if you attempt to hold on, you will lose that which you attempt to preserve, you will suffer in the process and you will die in the end.

It is precisely the tendency of life in the waking state to hold onto everything that is so damaging to the world. Give it all away and become part of the solution rather than continue on as part of the problem. Where your treasure is, there will your heart be also. If you store up your treasure where moth eats and rust corrupts, you will weep for your lost idols in the end, for one by one they will be taken from you. You will one day return to Life as you entered this world -- naked of body but trailing clouds of glory through your soul. Choose instead today for Truth and Beauty and for the Kingdom of Heaven -- not in some far off future state, but Here and Now -- and watch how quickly your life transforms in magic and wonder and love and joy.

Take these simple words to heart and I promise you, you will dance with the Ishayas in Immortal Life even here on Earth. Or deny us and run away -- it makes no difference to us but all the difference to you. So many rivers have flowed into the Unbounded Ocean before. The ocean needs none, accepts all, flatters none. Its status never changes - but what a transformation for the river! Its narrow boundaries fall away and are found no more. The river learns "I am the Ocean --" I am Infinite, Unbounded, Eternal. And this is known not as a dry, intellectual concept but as a vibrant, living Truth of what is.

Unite with us, children of Light and Truth and Joy, and we will transform this Earth in one generation into Paradise, back into the Garden of Eden. And we will find the Tree of the Knowledge of Good and Evil naturally transforms back into the Tree of Immortal Life. The abuses of the waking state will be universally replaced by the Direct Cognition of Perpetual Consciousness, in which every thought is based in permanent Infinite Awareness.

We stand on the threshold of a new age, an age prophesied in all parts of the world for thousands of years. The New

Jerusalem is at hand -- the twenty-seven Ascension Techniques are the master key to unlock all the boundaries of past painful choices and experiences and reveal the Unbounded Joy of life as it is.

Life is either a dancing adventure -- or nothing.
                                        -- Helen Keller

THE MIND

Awareness of the environment and our thoughts is the function of the mind. The mind is *not* the same thing as awareness: rather, it is a machine that is operated by awareness. The old belief that awareness is an artifact of the physical body is just a materialistic superstition and is falling rapidly away in the modern scientific and medical communities. The attempt to understand awareness as a by-product of chemical and electrical processes in neurons and nerve tissue was always doomed, for the source of our awareness is not the physical structure of our bodies. Awareness is primary; the body and the physical brain are secondary. The twelve billion cells of the central nervous system create the physical structure of the greatest computer of all time, but they are not themselves aware of anything, any more than the wires and circuitry of a computer are by themselves conscious.

The various functions of the physical mind are performed by an extremely complex network of interconnect-ed neurons: every neuron is connected to many thousands of others through direct synaptic connections and to millions or even billions of others through its receptor sites for neuropeptides. There are fifty trillion cells in the body; each is capable of producing the neuropeptides which communicate with the neurons in the brain. Thus the mind is not limited to the cerebral cortex; we are in fact body-minds -- the whole structure of our physiology is intelligent and capable of talking back and forth with itself. It is all alive with wisdom; it all reflects our individual awareness.

Memory and learning occur when we repeat a behavior enough that new neurological pathways are created. The more any action is repeated, the deeper the groove in the brain becomes: the more neurons are tied into the loop and the more the connections between them increase. When any behavior is thus locked into the physical structure of the body, the habits, beliefs and judgments that are associated with it become extremely hard to modify.

The self-sense that is our ego is built upon the groundwork of these mental structures. Although practical for much of life, the main trouble with these internal programs is that they keep us from fluidity of consciousness: we become stuck in old behaviors and beliefs and have a hard time in evolving new life and experience, for the mind resonates easily only with that which corresponds to previous impressions. New experience does not easily lodge if there is no similar internal pattern; the mind automatically filters out that which it cannot understand and discards it, particularly if the new information appears to pose a threat to the continuity of the ego.

Thus the cycle of action-experience-impression-desire continues and is difficult to break. An impulse of desire arises from the Ascendant, collides with a previous impression which colors the desire; the warped desire leads to action to fulfill itself; this action leads to an experience which strengthens the initial impression. The cycle can never be broken in its own Universe: there is no escape from action-experience-impression-desire on its own terms. What is required, of course, is a new program -- Ascension, for example, provides the means to rewrite the old internal structures effortlessly, for the mind opens to new experience along the path of increasing enjoyment.

Our experience of reality cannot be separated from the

beliefs, thoughts and perceptions of the mind. The major function of the mind is to create what it *thinks* is reality. The mind is like a mirror. If the glass of the mirror is dirty, the reflection is necessarily going to appear hazy or distorted. What is never experienced is the actual reality of anything, but only its resonance with our beliefs, judgments and inter- nal programs. What is this mirror? Without the reflection of objects, it vanishes. The mind can reflect anything, but without something to reflect, it is only awareness itself -- impossible to grasp by the intellect. The true nature of the mind's aware- ness can be experienced through systematic reduction of the reflection of thoughts and objects by Ascending, but it can never be understood by the rational faculties.

If we abuse the mind, we fall sick; if we use it as it was designed to be used, we find that physical and mental health are by-products of its natural style of functioning. As conscious awareness begins to expand as the result of Ascension, it becomes more and more obvious that most if not all the problems of life are rooted in the old destructive beliefs and judgments of projected desire and its opposite, projected aversion. Every mind is subject to misinterpretation of *everything* until the awareness of the Ascendant is stabilized.

The waking state is a collective hallucination. The hypnosis of the cultural conditioning of humanity is a result of the mind's inherent tendency to define or *name* everything.

Naming occurs when the mind organizes perceptions into an object, then assigns meaning to this mentally created object. This artificial reality is nothing more than an artifact of sensory perception; it is an out-picturing of a collection of images or concepts in the mind, it has no independent or external existence. Nothing exists in isolation from the value we assign to it. This is how the mind remains abstracted away from current experience: instead of seeing anything as it is, right Now, the mind sees only the past, or more accurately, only its previous beliefs and judgments about the past.

The waking state view of reality is that everything has independent existence. But what is that existence? If you take anything apart, you find that it no longer exists. Dismantle a computer, there is no computer left. "Computer" is just a name we have assigned onto an appearance, a collection of components.

External reality is phenomenal *only*. This is called *mithya* in Sanskrit. There is *something* outside which we call reality, but never what the mind has concluded it is. Each of us creates our own Universe based on our private interpretation of the changing flow of energies and appearances as they are per- ceived in our separate and isolated fragments of space and time.

The foundation of the entire belief system of the ego is in this waking state view of the universe. If things independently exist, then this "I" of the ego must also be independent and real. But the "I" is also simply a name -- it has no inherent reality.

When the old programs that sustain the waking state are rewritten, the energy that is locked in stress in the body is released. When this happens, the mirror of the mind is cleansed: the Clear Light of the Ascendant, the true nature of the mind, shines forth spontaneously. And then life begins to transform at a faster and faster pace. What contributes to this growth is letting go and flowing with the forces of Evolution; what detracts is attempting to hold onto the past. Holding onto the old behavior patterns and beliefs causes evolving life to suffer; letting go and falling into the new reality blossoming from inside creates joy. This is a simple choice, one much easier than is commonly realized. When one starts rapidly evolving, there may be tendencies from the old behavioral matrix -- from the environment, from past relationships, from old internal beliefs and patterns -- to resist the change. Guilt is often employed to keep change from occurring. "How could you do this to me?" is the cry of the embittered parts of the past. "How could you be so thoughtless, so uncaring?" It takes real dedication and commitment when challenged by the past in this way to stay firm with a new direction.

Though I speak in the tongues of men and of angels, but have not love, I am a noisy gong or a tinkling cymbal. And though I have the gift of prophecy, and understand all mysteries and all knowledge, and if I have all faith, so that I could remove mountains, but have not love, I am nothing. Though I give away all I have to feed the poor, and though I deliver my body to be burned, but have not love, I gain nothing.

Love never ends; as for prophecy, it will pass away; as for tongues, they will cease; as for knowledge, it will pass away. For our knowledge is imperfect and our prophecy is imperfect; but when the perfect comes, the imperfect will pass away.

When I was a child, I spoke like a child, I thought like a child, I reasoned like a child; when I became a man, I gave up childish ways. For now we see through a glass darkly, but then face to face. Now I know in part; then I shall understand fully, even as I have been fully understood.

So faith, hope, love abide, these three; but the greatest of these is love.

-- I Corinthians 13

V. ESCAPE FROM DARKNESS

Everything here is everywhere;
What is not here is nowhere at all.

This world is subject to manifold uncertainties. Making the human body secure is difficult or impossible. If it is not fed regularly, it starves. If it is not protected from the elements, it becomes ill or dies. It is subject to accidents: it can easily be crushed, broken, burned. There appears to be little or no possibility of living much beyond the century mark. Financial security is a chimera, shaky in the best of times. At any moment, the meaning and structure of our lives can be shaken to the core by death or illness of a loved one. This life is fundamentally uncertain. Even the most expensive defensive armaments can be surmounted, subverted, destroyed.

Given these obvious facts, what choice is there other than impotent frustration or despair? We shake our fist in rage at the cruel, judgmental God who created this horribly painful world. Joy is fleeting at best -- a stolen kiss, then the darkness and isolation of permanent loneliness or the dullness of blind, mindless fog. How many of us have chosen to eclipse our subtle perceptions to avoid seeing the ugly reality of Earth? How many of us dull our outraged senses with movies, television, videos, work, drugs, alcohol, or a countless series of other anodynes to still our pained and outraged sensibilities?

How many of us have ever dared question why? And for the rare seeker of Ultimate Knowledge, has not the result more often than not been the discovery that life is essentially meaningless? Is it a pointless drama created by a mad God? Or is it perhaps a random result of biochemical processes, inevitable somewhere, sometime in a nearly Infinite Universe?

How often does the seeker despair of independent discovery and adopt belief systems of others, be they religious, philosophical or scientific? Where is one who has succeeded in knowing the True Self, the Inner Controller, the Divine Mind?

Our senses lie to us. Our thought systems structured by sensory experience, logic or belief are necessarily flawed if we take as premise anything we perceive as ultimately real. Life is not the result of a consensus of opinion. It is not dependent on our sensory experience, our rational thought or on our beliefs.

Our senses lie to us. Every day we see the Sun rising in the East, setting in the West. This was incontrovertible fact for countless millennia to the vast majority of humanity. The Sun circled the flat Earth. Everybody knew that. But the perception was false; the logical and scientific systems based on the observations were flawed; the religious and philosophical systems based on this common daily experience were in error.

Our senses lie to us. For centuries, the indivisible nature of matter was accepted as gospel. But what rational mind today doubts that matter is only congealed energy? Most of that which we consider solid is 99.9999% empty space! Take an atom and expand it to the size of the Louisiana Super Dome and where is the matter? A tiny beebee sized lump in the center is the nucleus, containing the protons and neutrons; a few infinitesimal ghosts flitter around the outer bleachers, these are the electrons; all the rest is empty space. Where is the solid matter?

Our senses lie to us. What we have come to believe, based on our experiences, may not necessarily be true. Our knowledge of the world is changing at an ever-accelerating rate. That which was certain fact yesterday is today questioned and may be refuted tomorrow. The sum total of human knowledge is doubling every two years. Who is abreast of its discoveries? Who, indeed even can be abreast of its discoveries?

It is common today to view our scientific achievements with pride; some of us therefore feel contempt for the woefully ignorant philosophical and religious systems of previous generations. This is human nature. But it is just another level of ignorance.

AN EXPERIMENT FOR LIFE

If you like, here is an experiment you could try. It takes just a little of your time and can be productive of great good. For one brief moment, imagine that *everything* you now believe about the human condition and the world around you is wrong. Imagine every conclusion you have ever made is false, that you have been and are dreaming. Imagine no one you know has ever died, that it was all a magical drama created just for you. Imagine no one has even ever been ill, that no one has suffered in any way. Imagine the memories you have of your own pain are false, that you have never and never can suffer in any way, that you have simply been asleep and dreaming strange fantasies.

A peculiar thought? Astounding in the extreme? You strongly maintain you know many who have suffered intensely and died? You yourself may have certain chronic ailments or several self-destructive habits; you yourself have experienced losses, disappointments, injuries -- these are the irrefutable facts of your life. So how can I ask you even to imagine such a flawless world? A world without pain, suffering, loss of any kind? Perhaps such a place was possible in the far distant past or will be in some obscure future, but it is certainly not here and now. Or perhaps in a distant star system, a highly fortunate race has developed such a state of perfection, through intense scientific or spiritual development. Perhaps technology may one day eliminate all human suffering. Or maybe it will never happen on the Earth, maybe such a state will forever be reserved for the blessed ones in Heaven who, after death, have been judged worthy of Eternal Life. Perhaps then the Omnipotent Healing Strength of the Divine Hands will lovingly brush away all our tears and we will be reborn in the perfection and dazzling radiance of our own released Ascendant beauty.

But surely not here. Surely not now. It is impossible, illogical, and refuted by every scrap of evidence that our belief systems and memories and perceptions provide.

But again I say, what if? What if all the suffering you and others experienced was a cunning lie, an illusion created by a belief in separation from your own perfected Self? What happens to the pain in the dream when you wake up? If it had been a particularly painful dream, you might give a little shudder of relief that it was after all only a series of hallucinations. And then, thankful to be free from the terror, your racing heart stills as you continue joyfully on with your everyday life.

Let us be bold for just a moment longer and take this experiment one step further. Think of a past pain. It can be as large as you like. A severe burn. A broken arm or leg. Some disease that afflicted you. The death of a close one. Anything at all. Pick something that still hurts. Something that is still deep and painful. The betrayal by him/her whom you loved/trusted the most in all the world. The Holocaust. Viet Nam.

Pick this old-new pain and feel it now. What is that pain? What exactly is it? What does it feel like? *What is pain?* Can you describe it to yourself?

If you were to jab yourself with a pin just now, what would you feel? Your senses would relay a message to your brain through the wonderful electrical and chemical mechanics of your nervous system; these messages you would interpret to say, "Ouch!" And everybody knows exactly how that feels -- we have all had such experiences, we all have had such shared perceptions. But what *is* pain? *What exactly is it?* If you wish to be free from suffering permanently, this warrants investigation.

There is another way to view the world, based neither on intellectual enquiry nor belief but on direct experience. If you were happy before the pinprick -- if you just received a long-desired promotion or just discovered an ideal girlfriend or boyfriend, or just received an "A" in a difficult class -- you will still feel the pin, but the pain will seem much less important. If, on the other hand, you just got fired, broke up with your fiancée, flunked algebra, the jab from the pin will feel much worse. You might wonder in response to the prick why God created such a miserable world. You might curse your fate. You might kick your dog or slam your dinner down on the table or just scream your anger and frustration to the uncaring world.

Suppose you are running a foot-race, say a ten kilometer race, for which you have trained for a long time. You are about to win when another competitor comes up from behind you and trips you; you fall down together and both lose. How will you feel about this? If you are like most of us, you will probably be extremely angry.

But suppose he did not trip you intentionally but was at the time suffering a severe myocardial infarction -- he was having a massive heart attack. What happens to your anger now? Is it not replaced by pity or sadness for the poor unfortunate fellow? The same event has now been interpreted completely differently, with vastly different effects on your moods and feelings.

Now suppose you learn he had the heart attack because he had been taking illegal drugs so he could win the race. Once again, your feelings transform, spiralling again into anger, with a strong touch of judgment and condemnation thrown in to salt the feeling. "He *deserved* to die!" you think, happy for his demise. Or perhaps you still feel some pity for him, thinking it sad that he wanted to win so badly. And you offer this to yourself as proof that moral behavior is rewarded.

But next you discover that he was a foreign national and his wife, parents and children were being held prisoner by the dictator of his country; further this dictator had told him that if he won the race, his family would be freed, but if he lost, they would be executed slowly and painfully. Now what happens to your feelings? Where did the anger go? Maybe it transfers to anger toward the dictator or toward politics or toward God for making such a senseless, cruel world. But what of your anger for the poor dead athlete? Who could condemn him now?

Our interpretation of reality is everything. We have many good reasons for all of our feelings, but the fact is that our moods change like the seasons: at one minute we are filled with love and joy, at the next, we know only hatred, pain and fear. And in every case, we feel completely justified in our feelings, *based on our interpretation of reality*.

The principle in operation is that the world is as we perceive it. There are fundamental differences in degrees of consciousness from person-to-person and even from moment-to- moment within each of us. Some days we feel better than other days, some days we feel less burdened, some days we are more creative, happier, more at peace with ourselves and with our Universe.

There are countless degrees of consciousness available to every human. There is a state of conscious where all is still and dark and the conscious mind thinks of nothing. This we call sleeping. There is another state where we are limited only by our imaginations; absolutely anything we can conceive occurs. This we call dreaming. And there is the state we call waking, structured by certain definite physical laws, in which life is quite predictable. This is a state where if you place your hand in fire, you will be burned, where if you step unprotected off the top of a fifty-story building, you will surely die. Pain, suffering and ineluctable death are the eternal handmaidens of life in the waking state.

But the waking state *is* subject to variation. Anything that changes is not permanent, it is not eternal. We can at least conceive of lives with little pain and suffering, even if death in the end is the final result. What might the limit of such variations be? What is the potential of human life? Is there a limit? Most would agree that there have been "great souls" on this planet -- individuals who are so far beyond the standard that we revere them as being enlightened, saints, geniuses, or even God incarnate. Is it that there are only a gifted few who are capable of deeper thought, perception, understanding and love? Or does everyone have this potential, and is it simply not developed in the average person?

There are many ancient traditions in the world that maintain that anyone can rise to complete human consciousness, that anyone can live the highest state of human development. Far from being the exclusive privilege of the chosen few, blessed by birth or circumstance, these traditions claim this is the natural birthright of all.

If this is true, it must not be difficult to move into a more expanded level of consciousness. It must be neither complicated nor a matter of faith. It must not require a giant intellect nor an unswerving belief. Nothing must be required that is not possessed by all humans everywhere. The only requirements would be curiosity and the willingness to give this development a chance.

How curious. This well describes the practice of Ascension as taught by the Ishayas.

OPENING THE DOOR

The rewards of the development of consciousness are limitless -- every area of life is beneficially affected by the growth of full human awareness. There is no problem, physical, emotional, mental or spiritual that cannot be reduced and eventually resolved as an individual moves more and more toward complete consciousness.

Why this must be so may not be immediately clear. The problems of life are multi-fold and extreme. How can any one thing affect all areas of life?

Consider our daystar. The Sun, a thermonuclear fusion fire some 96 million miles from the Earth, brings light to all Earth's creatures by day, chasing the darkness from every corner of our lives.

Just so, there is a light within our minds, a light we variously call our consciousness, our spirit, our Self, our soul. This inner awareness acts in our individual lives like the Sun acts for our Earth. This inner consciousness is the root of the tree of our life, the basis of all that we think, all that we perceive, all that we feel, all that we do. Calling the inner light the root of the tree of our life is reminiscent of the metaphorical passage in the Bible about Eden and the Tree of Life and the Tree of the Knowledge of Good and Evil.

This passage, as so much of the world's scripture, has been interpreted from the waking state of consciousness --

with rather unfortunate results. The Tree in either case -- as the Tree of Life *or* as the Tree of the Knowledge of Good and Evil -- is the human nervous system. When it is used properly, it functions as the Tree of Life, bringing health and life and all good things to the human being. When the human ego (the serpent) is drawn into the experience of duality, the emotional nature (Eve principle) eats of the apple of duality, and the rational mind (Adam principle) follows -- the individual perceives duality, feels hot and cold, believes in good and bad. In this state, the nervous system loses its innocent perception of immortality and becomes the Tree of the Knowledge of Good and Evil. In this state of judging, dualistic life necessarily ends in death. A house divided against itself cannot long endure. It will rot, it will decay, it will fall. If we live by the two-edged sword of judgment, we will surely die by it.

It is not difficult to restore the proper functioning of the nervous system -- it is only necessary to take the poisoned apple of duality back out of the mouth. To do this, the requirement is to stop listening to the serpent, the desires of the ego that lead in the direction of duality. There are two voices inside every human -- the first speaks for the ego and leads to judgment, to fear, to defense, to the continuance of ignorance; the second speaks for the Ascendant and leads to clear perception, to love, to invincibility, to Self-realization.

If the inner light of awareness becomes stronger in us, all dark areas, all problems of every kind naturally begin to vanish, as if by magic. It takes no great expenditure of energy, no in-depth or complicated working to solve the problems of individual life; they are simply no more found. Allegorically speaking, we could say that the Kingdom of Heaven is at hand. It is Here, it is Now. No time needs to elapse to realize this. It is not necessary to spend years in meditation or prayer, it is not necessary to purify the body or mind to awaken to this Truth. Each of us is already conscious! We have already been given everything we need to be perfect, even as our Father in Heaven is perfect. Where is Heaven? It is here, close by, directly at hand, in our heart. Who is our Father in Heaven? He is here, close by, directly at hand, in our heart: He is our most expanded or developed level of consciousness, our own perfected Eternal Self. God, being all love, creates only in His own image and likeness. We, created by God, must therefore be only all love.

What happens to the darkness of the night when the Sun rises? Where does it go? What happens to our dreams when we awaken? Where do they go? In a sense they are destroyed, in a sense the darkness is vanquished with the Ascendancy of the light, but this is a rather odd perspective. Why focus on the fate of the shadows and the illusions when we can instead rejoice in the glory of the rising Sun? Let us celebrate our enlightenment, not bemoan the loss of our ignorance.

As the Sun of consciousness rises in the mind, every shadow area of life naturally retreats without our having to worry about it. Nothing can stop this, it is coming to all; nothing can even much slow it except attempting to hold onto our ancient rigid beliefs. The day comes; this is inevitable, as certain as life; night ends. It is a perfectly natural and unavoidable process. Once begun, the process continues until it is complete.

Who can stop the Sun from rising? There is a certain fortunate inevitability about natural processes. Once the light of Infinite Consciousness starts to dawn, it is difficult to delay this process. In fact, it is much easier for the nervous system to function in the state of full consciousness (as the Tree of Life); it is quite remarkable in retrospect that the waking state with its myriad of judgments and beliefs (the Tree of Good and Evil) is so tenacious in its hold on the mind. How can any finite boundaries of thought and feeling hold back Infinite Awareness? It is odd, peculiar, strange and takes a tremendous expenditure of energy every day for this to continue. Wasting so much energy every day is exhausting -- as mentioned before, this is why it is necessary to sleep at night; this is why bodies fall ill, age and die. So much of our human energy is devoted to avoiding the direct perception of Reality.

Why do we do this? Primarily because we fear, at a deep level in the mind, the alternative! We are terrified of knowing who we are! The ego has absolutely convinced us that to know who we are means the loss of our individuality. We believe that to let go will mean that we are absorbed in a unity that will steal away our self. It is not so! What we gain is our Universal, Cosmic Self. But to the ego, this is fear, this is death, this is damnation eternal.

Who wants to go to a heaven where the most exciting thing to do is play the same kind of harp and everybody looks the same and everything is equal? Few people I know. And yet this is what the ego would have us believe enlightenment is like.

THE SOURCE OF DARKNESS

Why do we avoid our inner growth into Self knowledge as if it were the plague? The first answer is habit: it is our beliefs and judgments about the nature of life that hold us back. This is true, as far as it goes. But why are our habits so frightfully gripping to the mind? If the power of the Ascendant truly is Omnipotent, how can there be a challenge from anywhere to this Absolute Force?

Logically, there cannot be. There could be no dark energy that could challenge Infinite Strength, even for a millisecond of a millisecond. And if there could be one for that long, even that could be nothing more than an illusory challenge.

If we face away from the Sun, we will cast a shadow. If we never turn to face the light, we may learn to believe, based on our own personal experience, that the shadows are real. But of what importance the shadows if suddenly we turn around and face the Sun? At first, our eyes may be dazzled after so long spent struggling to discern differences in the darkness. But as they grow accustomed to their natural function, it becomes increasingly difficult, even impossible to see shadows lurking in the darkness, for there no longer is any darkness.

The light of Infinite Consciousness resides within each of us. This *must* be so, else it would not be Infinite. We are all sparks of the divine flame -- we are all creations of the Ascendant, sharing in the characteristics of the Ascendant -- Infinite light, Unbounded joy, perfect peace, undying love, immortal life. It is only our continual, moment-by-moment decision to remain with our backs to the light that keeps us lost in the darkness.

This is a better answer than habit. It is *our choice* to face the darkness of duality or the light of unity. The human comes equipped with free will as part of our birthright. We are made in the image of the Ascendant in every respect. At any second, we can turn back to reclaim our heritage.

This may sound surprising, for the initial choice for separation from the light was made so long ago that most of us have only the dimmest of recollections of our previous, light-saturated state of being.

In retrospect, it is easy to see why vast energy is required to maintain that age-old decision. The Infinite light of consciousness pervades every particle of space and time, every atom in the Universe, every cell in our bodies. Difficult indeed it is to keep the Infinite at bay. Tremendous expenditure of energy is continually required; this proves exceedingly tiring to the typical mind, hastens the decay and eventual destruction of the body, causes as corollary an impressive array of physical, emotional and mental problems. "Impressive" because of the enormous size of the list, not because of the magnitude of the problems.

Since every problem on Earth is traceable to the one fact that each of us is making a continual, moment-by-moment decision to turn from the light, then all problems must be identical. No problem can be any larger or smaller than another, and any one can be as easily cured as any other.

This may seem to fly in the face of common sense. How can terminal cancer or death itself be equated with the common cold or with the fact that our husband brought his boss home for dinner without notice? If there were truly no difference in problems, the entire range of human despair and frustration would appear identical to the enlightened!

This is in fact true. Christ could heal the sick and raise the dead because he had fully realized all problems are illusions born exactly in the same way -- by turning away from the Infinite light of the Ascendant. He realized he could unmake these mistaken perceptions by knowing that all problems are caused in the same way, by belief in duality.

Said another way, the true Healer perceives illness and death as nothing more or less than illusions in the mind of the sufferer. If the Healer is free from illusions, it becomes possible to help those who are still caught by their ancient and yet continuous decision. By representing the Truth for the sick, the Healer heals. The Healer sees only the Truth: the sufferer *is* well, a perfect representation of the Ascendant on Earth. If the

sick one chooses to share this perception, change the mind and
turn back to the inner light, healing is instantaneous. Only
belief in duality stands in error. And the nice thing about any
belief is that it can be changed, based on new experience.

I am not recommending we stand before someone who
is ill and say with judgment, "Your illness is an illusion, get up
and be well!" Nor am I recommending that we act in such a silly
way to ourselves. It is not by adopting a new belief system that
our old beliefs fall. It is by learning to experience a different
reality that our beliefs change. Only a new tree will grow a new
fruit. If the old tree is growing poisoned apples of despair,
sickness and death, a new tree is required to produce a new
harvest of joy, health and life.

This is why this book is rather short by modern-day
standards. Talking about the Infinite light is not the same as
experiencing it. Thinking about chocolate does not provide the
taste of chocolate. Picking this book up, reading it and saying,
"Gosh, that sounds interesting," and then putting it back on the
shelf without attempting to discover the Truth of what is
written here is manifesting yet another branch of the lunacy
that afflicts most people in the world today. This is not a book
about Reality! This is an open invitation to *experience* Reality.
Perhaps by now the difference should be beginning to become
obvious.

There is so much that is disappointing in the modern
world. So many promises have been made only to be broken.
Some people have become so highly discouraged that even
when they stumble across a True path that does lead to
enlightenment, they have grown so jaded and cynical that they
can't even follow the simplest instructions and wander away
after a day or so. In teaching Ascension, we have occasionally
met such sad souls. After an hour or two or perhaps a day or a

week of feebly attempting to reverse their life-long habits of useless belief, they run away from Ascension in terror. In terror of what? The transformation that results from turning to look at the light. The fact that they rarely or never realize that this is why they run is just one more example of how the illusory ego keeps life chained into the most absurd and limited boundaries of experience.

How can there be any distance at all to be traversed? It is an infinitesimally small turning of awareness inside, an extremely simple and direct reversal of an ancient decision. "The Kingdom of Heaven is at Hand," is an absolutely correct statement. It doesn't say that the Kingdom of Heaven will be someday in the future after you have done thus and so for x amount of time. No, Heaven is *Here*, it is *Now*. "My name is I AM." It is not "I will be," or "I was." The present instant is exactly that -- present, here, now! As such, no technique is needed, no master is required, no great and enduring faith or years of painstaking study are required. The return to your home, your perfect inner light, need take no time, no years of practice, no lifetimes of gradual progress with unshakable dedication.

There is an ancient story which illustrates this point rather well.

One day, God came walking through the world to see how his children were faring. He came upon an old ascetic who had spent his entire adult life in severe bodily mortification and forceful mental disciplines.

The ascetic had gained a certain degree of clarity of his senses from his prolonged practice and realized that the man casually walking by his cave was fully established in awareness of the inner Divine Self. Painfully unwinding his body from his rigid posture, the ascetic bowed before God and said, "Great-Souled One! I perceive you are an illumined master. Pray tell me, honorable sir, how long it will be before I realize my inner Divine

Nature?"

God smiled warmly and laughingly replied, "You are doing well, my son! At your present rate of progress, you will realize your inner Divine Self with just one more lifetime of similar effort."

The ascetic, terrified, in shock, cried, "Another lifetime of this horror? How can I endure this boredom, this agony, this pain for another day, let alone another lifetime! How horrible! You have cursed me this day! Begone from this place, you imposter! Never would I believe such as you."

God smiled lovingly at him and walked on. Soon He came upon an idiot splashing in the river, laughing and singing. This man's primary activity every day was to cry out, "God! How I love God! God! I love God! God!" This foolish one never took the slightest care for his physical needs, never cared if he were fed, clothed, housed. He never noticed if he were clean or dirty, hot or cold, wet or dry. He might have been locked up in a padded cell in our modern age, but in those days, people saw that he was harmless and therefore tolerated him and occasionally gave him a crust of bread or some old, half-rotten fruits or vegetables to eat.

This idiot was attracted by the radiance of this handsome stranger, came up out of the water, bowed before him and said, "How wonderful! God has sent by a Great-Souled One. I have been enjoying myself so much of late I had nearly forgotten I have a goal. I began my quest to realize enlightenment long ago but of late have become distracted by this constant joy welling up inside. Seeing you just now reminded me of my journey and I was wondering if you could tell me how long it will be before I realize my inner Divine Nature?"

God smiled warmly and laughingly replied, "You are doing well, my son! At your present rate of progress, you will realize your inner Divine Self with just seventy more lifetimes of similar effort."

"Seventy lifetimes of similar effort!" cried the idiot with perfect joy. "How wonderful! What a flawless boon, you have today bestowed upon me, Great Lord!" The idiot was so filled with joy at the prospect of another seventy lifetimes of such bliss that the last doubt fled from his mind; his last question melted into the joy that was his life; his ignorance was irrevocably crushed; he attained the highest state of enlightenment instantly.

> Tell me not, in mournful numbers,
>   "Life is but an empty dream!"
> For the soul is dead that slumbers,
> And things are not what they seem.
>
> Life is real! life is earnest!
>   and the grave is not its goal.
> "To dust thou art to dust returneth"
>   was not spoken of the soul.
>
> In the world's broad field of battle,
>   In the bivouac of Life
> Be not like dumb, driven cattle!
>   Be a hero in the strife!
>
> Lives of great men all remind us
> We can make our lives sublime,
> And, departing, leave behind us
> Footprints on the sands of time.

-- *Longfellow*

VI. LOVE

My Name is "I AM."

We on Earth commonly think there are three kinds of time: the past, the present and the future. We often guide our actions largely on the basis of regret for our past actions and missed opportunities or from concern for our future well-being. The problem with living for the future is that the future never arrives. It doesn't exist except as an invented concept. There is only NOW -- now extends in all places and at all times. The past does not exist, either: there was, before this instant, an unbroken succession of Now moments; there will be in the future an unbroken succession of Now moments. Now, the present, is the only time there is, the only time there has ever been, the only time there ever will be.

This is why it is so absurdly easy to gain enlightenment -- the Infinite light is already here, now, within the grasp of each of us. Nothing more is required than ceasing the attempt to live in the past or the future. The Sun is always shining; we have only to stop identifying with the clouds passing in front of it to be free.

The unhappy ascetic was not enjoying the present; he was continually hoping to realize his Self in the future. Therefore the prospect of even one more moment of such torture was agonizing. The happy idiot, on the other hand, thoroughly enjoyed each and every instant -- he was filled with joy at the thought of continuing his ecstatic present. The additional rush of joy through his already bliss-saturated nervous system was more than the last of his ego's weakened belief system could withstand -- the old limitations in his mind, already largely discarded, were destroyed -- the Infinite light of the Now burst through him, upward and out, transforming his life permanently. His eyes fully opened for the first time; he recognized God standing before him. The newly enlightened one bowed before his Lord and cried his gratitude and joy to the Source of all that is.

We human beings have an unfortunate habit of unnecessarily complicating our lives. Love is supremely simple, absolutely fundamental, requires no training whatsoever, is permanently transforming, increases more and more as it is given away, and is the greatest secret in the entire Universe. Like most great secrets, this particular one is displayed openly, as if it were valueless. It is here for all who wish to have it; there is no limited supply; it increases from age to age and yet is Infinitely full always.

What stands between any of us and the full experience and expression of love? In fact, nothing at all. Love is the most natural expression of everyone's life, the one fundamental constituent of everything, the innermost basis of every feeling of every being in created time. It is simpler to experience love for everyone than to experience any dark emotion, any feeling of hatred or fear. Why, then, is the world apparently dying from lack of love? What abuse of industry, government, disease, crime or neglect could not be cured by just a drop more comprehensive vision inspired by the smallest increase in love? The world is being strangled by the absence of love! Where the all-embracing wonder of life, where the overpowering joy in this? Why is the world so sick?

I visited a garden in Charlotte today. It was small, little more than three acres, but beauty was everywhere. The couple that created it bought the lot in 1927 -- at the time, it was treeless, a red clay-baked North Carolina cornfield; now their Wing Haven is considered one of the loveliest gardens in the region. It is a garden famous not only for its inherent loveliness but also for the multitudes of wild birds that live and visit there. The founders' manifest love transformed this one-time barren field into a little slice of wonder.

This couple was not inherently different from anyone else, with the single exception that they had a deep intuitive grasp of one of the most fundamental principles of the enlightened -- if you want to experience love, give love.

This Earth is not loveless. On the contrary, it is saturated with love overflowing everywhere at all times. Those who are desperately lonely and love-starved are living in an artificial hell of their own creation. They are lonely and love-starved only because they demand that everyone else prove they love them first.

I once had a friend, I'll call him Mike Little, who was talented in many areas: he was a talented classical guitarist, a great dancer, a brilliant conversationalist, a gifted astrologer. But Mike could never maintain a relationship with a person of the opposite sex for more than a few days. I asked him once why he thought this was so. His answer was, I thought, quite revealing: "No one can love better than I can. I know this! But I'm waiting for the perfect girl before I reveal my love."

"How will you recognize her?" I asked, fascinated. "Does she have a particular appearance?"

"Oh no, nothing superficial like that. The perfect girl will love me first! She will be willing to give herself to me completely. She will open her heart fully to me. Such a hidden diamond she will get in me! I know how deeply I can love. She will be so lucky!"

How often do we think in similar ways? "If only he would stop smoking/drinking/doing drugs/get a regular job be nicer to me/love my mother more/be nicer to my children - - why then, I would give him my whole heart." It is easy to see, when it is presented like this, how completely upside down this kind of thinking is. Love second, you will wait forever to be loved. Love first, you will be loved. This is absolutely guaranteed.

There is another similar kind of thinking, closely allied to it. This kind demands proof of love to love back. It usually goes like this: "Jacki said she loves me. But if she truly loves me, she would. . ." and then we fill in the blanks with whatever it is we want from Jacki or believe Jacki should do for us to demonstrate her love. We have a deeply rooted habit of defining others' love for us in specific ways that fit neatly with our romantic ideal, which is a creation of that part of our minds that likes to dwell in fantasies and/or the future.

But there are no absolute standards of behavior. Being loved by someone does not imply that the lover must conform to any particular rigid standards we might desire.   On the contrary, if the love is mutual, freedom of expression naturally increases. Many people in our society feel that being in love means putting the partner in a cage -- controlled, defined, restricted, bound. This most often happens when the male member of the relationship overshadows and dominates the female. But occasionally it is seen in reverse.

There could be a great many reasons for desiring and attempting to enslave another, but typically this behavior results from a sense of insecurity -- "Mary would find someone else and leave me if I didn't watch her closely." --- "John would betray me if I didn't keep him on a tight leash." And so forth.

Again, a sense of insecurity can have many different causes, based on previous experience -- "My father was killed on the freeway when I was sixteen." -- "My mother left me for three weeks with my aunt when I was four." -- "My wife ran away with a vacuum cleaner salesman." The list is as long as the life-experiences of the human race. But any sense of insecurity *always* reduces down to a deep-rooted sense of unworthiness.

If I don't feel I am worthy of love, I will structure my life (quite unconsciously) to prove that I am not loved. Again and again I will demonstrate the truth of my own self-image. Then I will be able to say to others and to myself, "See, it didn't work out because he/she just didn't love me enough. It's not my fault. I am quite innocent. He/she betrayed me."

Taking personal responsibility for the parts of our lives that don't work to our satisfaction can be one of the more difficult parts of assuming control of our own destiny. Yet this is also one of the most important. If we condemn anyone else for anything at all, we are projecting our own guilt and lack of worthiness onto the world. It is difficult or impossible to see anything outside that does not exist inside. Rabbits live in a rabbit world, not a bird's. Dogs live in a Dog Universe, not our human one.

If an angel comes to your door and you don't believe in angels, what will you see? If you believe that everyone is out to get you, how will you greet anyone you don't know? If you believe everyone is basically untrustworthy, how can you ever hope to trust anyone? In large cities, we walk by thousands of strangers every day. We have become so inured to their presence we frequently don't even glance at them. They could be smiling with joy to see us, but we don't look up from our private world to greet them. This is not just true on busy pedestrian thoroughfares, it carries over to our silent and sparsely populated pathways in our public parks. We are walking alone; another person approaches us; we pass each other without sharing a single glance or a word. How often this occurs every day! Of what are we so terrified? Is every stranger a criminal? If we dare to smile or take a dangerous plunge and say, "Hello!" are we going to be mugged or raped on the spot? We act as if we believe this were so.

The basic principle at work is that the Universe perfectly reflects back to us our beliefs and understandings about life. This is partially a result of our human physiology -- we don't see as well as hawks, smell as well as dogs, hear as well as dolphins -- but the range of the senses operating within our own species is primarily a result of our belief systems and the experiences we have accumulated based on those belief systems.

THE POWER OF BELIEF

We don't often recognize how powerful and subtle our beliefs are. We don't normally think that our nearsightedness is primarily a product of deeply rooted racial, societal or familial conviction and only secondarily a result of physical factors. We don't believe that our minds control our bodies and not the other way around. And yet, there have been well documented cases of multiple-personality individuals in which one of the occupying personalities believes he/she can see perfectly well and requires no glasses and another believes that he/she cannot see properly and is nearly blind without artificial correction. The personality in dominance at any given time determines how well the physical eyes work!

In another case, one sub-personality is allergic to oranges and breaks out in hives whenever one is eaten; another loves oranges and eats them without the slightest side effect. We normally dismiss these cases as being bizarre or extraordinary and have little bearing on our individual lives. And yet how many of us have conflicting personalities inside that deeply influence our behavior?

We commonly feel that the body and mind are separate entities -- there are physical problems and there are mental problems; they are distinct. But the body-mind is actually more of a continuum -- the physical structure is a congealed expression of our habitual patterns of thinking and believing. The body is secondary, a tool of the mind, not the other way around. The body has no power in and by itself to do anything. It cannot be sick or injured without the consent of the mind.

Is this a difficult idea to grasp? Our standard world-view holds that the mind is limited by the body, which is primary. If we are accustomed to think of our minds as bound by our bodies, then it will be particularly hard to unravel this concept. But if we could, even for an instant, relax our beliefs and judgments, we would find that there are other ways of viewing the mind and the mind-body relationship -- and these other ways might serve us much better.

If the individual changes his/her mind, the body responds accordingly. Thus a physical "miracle" such as a sudden reversal of disease or injury is, simply, a deep change of mind in the healed person. It is not a change of mind in the Healer. The Healer is already healed. This explains why so many prayers for healing are seemingly not answered -- healing *never* comes from the outside in -- it *always* comes from the inside out. The God-force within can heal anyone of anything. If you can recognize your inner Divine Nature, perfect health is the automatic result. God on the outside, however, as an external force disconnected from your innermost being would be denying your free will if It healed you. Created in the image of God means created with Absolute freedom of choice. This is abrogated never. First you must change your mind and desire perfect health. Then healing occurs. Then, in fact, healing *must* occur -- it is the automatic by-product of who you are. But the change of mind must be on the deepest level of your being -- simply deciding with the surface mind that "I am well" is not only useless but potentially mentally deranging. Affirmations repeated by the conscious thinking level of the mind, although occasionally soothing distraught emotional states, are all but worthless for bringing about a deep transformation of perception of Reality. An affirmation repeated a few times a day does little to counteract the intensity of the habitual patterns created by the average adult human's 50,000 daily thoughts.

It may appear easier to change your mind about "small" illnesses than about major, life-threatening diseases. You may have no difficulty in conquering the common cold -- you may not have been sick in years and years -- but suddenly you develop cancer and see no alternative but chemotherapy or radiation.

Some conceptions of disease are more deeply rooted in ourselves and in the collective consciousness of humanity than are others. The more fundamental and universal the belief in the particular disease or injury, the more profound must be your understanding that you are incapable of being sick or injured if you desire to be well.

A doctor friend of mine once told me a curious story that illustrates how the body's state of health is based on the mind's beliefs. This doctor was approached by a sweet little old lady complaining of severe abdominal pains. Upon examination, the doctor concluded that exploratory surgery was indicated, as this unfortunate soul most likely had cancer of the colon.

Upon opening her up, the doctor did indeed find an extremely advanced case of cancer -- it had metastasized to several organs and was inoperable. The doctor gave her three weeks at the most to live. Sadly sewing her up, he debated whether or not to tell her this awful truth. He tried but simply couldn't force himself to do it; instead, he told her she had only had gallstones, which he had removed. Deeply saddened by the failure of his science, he bade the kind old woman farewell, knowing he would never see her again.

Imagine his amazement when a year later this woman walked into his office, vibrantly healthy, to tell him how alive and happy she had felt ever since her operation! The doctor examined her and found not the slightest trace of the dread disease. Mystified, he asked her if she had had any unusual experiences since he had last seen her.

"No," she replied, "but I must tell you! When I came to see you, I was so afraid I had cancer. When you explained it was only gallstones, I was so relieved and happy that I resolved never to be ill another day in my life."

A strange coincidence? An unlikely and rare healing without known cause? Most doctors encounter such infrequent events from time to time, but having no physical explanation, they choose to ignore them, filing them under the general catch-all category of "spontaneous (and therefore unexplainable) remissions."

What do you think?

VII. THE SOURCE OF ALL THAT IS

There never was a time when I was not,
nor you, nor these rulers of men,
nor will there ever be a time when all of us
will cease to be.
-- The Bhagavad Gita

The most ancient philosophies of the Earth declare that the human race is far older than our histories have recorded, vastly older than our archaeologists, paleontologists and anthropologists have even begun to dream. Throughout the long history of the Universe, self-conscious beings have always existed. "Self-conscious beings" is the only definition of humanity that is consistent or meaningful. How many feet high, how many feet wide, how many arms or legs or heads, any and all physical attributes are much too trivial to define what it means to be human.

If this is so, the debate about whether or not our present physical form is descended from a prototype ape-like being is ultimately irrelevant. If we evolved from a lower form of life is not important for our growth to enlightenment; what is important is that we realize we are all manifestations of and remain connected to the Source of all that is. This Source has been called many things. Any name for it is just fine, for the Source is impossible to offend. But because so many names for the Source have become associated with belief systems, and some of these belief systems have become associated with fear or are in other ways distorted by the ego, in this Teaching, the Ishayas usually call this Original Prime Force the Ascendant.

The Ascendant is the sum total of everything that is. It is the Source and the Essence and the Goal of all that lives. This entire enormous Universe of one thousand billion galaxies (each containing an average of one hundred billion stars) is a part -- a small part -- of the Ascendant. Every human that exists, every human that has ever existed or ever will exist is a part of the Ascendant. Every plant, every animal, every grain of sand, every particle of energy, every impulse of rational thought, every emotion, every single thing in every level of creation is included within the Ascendant. There are no exceptions. Everything everywhere at every time, past, present or future, is part of the Ascendant. There has never been nor will there ever be anything anywhere that is not part of the Ascendant.

Most people can, at least intellectually, grasp such a concept. But most also have a hard time conceiving of what this really means. And yet if an individual could do so, even for an instant, that individual would find his or her life permanently altered.

Modern physics is beginning to demonstrate that there exists an ultimately abstract Universal Reality. All of matter is reducible to energy; at the finest levels of creation, energy is infinitely powerful and present everywhere. The ground state of quantum mechanics is universal, Omnipresent, bursting with Infinite creative energy and the source of all that is. This whole enormous Universe came from an area measuring 10^{-43} centimeters in an instant of time fifteen to twenty billion years ago, or so we are told.

But what modern physics has not revealed to us is that this substratum of creation is in fact open to human awareness. There is not now, there has never been, there will never be a human who cannot experience the Ascendant. The state of health of the physical body is not relevant; the state of health of the mental body -- the intellect, mind and the emotions -- is not relevant, the belief systems, habits and judgments about life, none of these are relevant. There are *no* requisites for experience of the Ascendant, the Universal Source of all that is.

And yet, few do consciously experience Universal Mind. And if one is lucky to have a fleeting glimpse into the workings of the Ascendant, typically the glimpse is short and quickly shrouded. Why, if the Ascendant is present everywhere, and if anyone anywhere at any time *can* experience it, why is it that so few consciously do? Why have so many of those who have believed in the existence of the Ascendant believed also that it is difficult to attain it? Why have many felt that it takes years of arduous effort and even then a great deal of luck to succeed? The Eastern literature is filled with the extraordinary hardship considered necessary to realize enlightenment, full conscious communion with the Ascendant. And in the West, the "dark night of the Soul" has been thought to be the usual lot of the Christian lover of God -- a rare and fleeting taste of the Divine is followed by the inevitable re-immersion in the tragic fog of the Earth-life of the senses. It is believed that it is the lot of the seeker of Truth to be cursed by earthly desires, enslaved by matter and doomed to a most frustrating life. No wonder so few anymore seek the goal! Why spend years on a doubtful quest when the end result is so unlikely?

Rare indeed anywhere on the globe has been the fully realized sage, the enlightened sorceress, nagual, priest, magician, saint -- the name for those in conscious contact with the Ascendant has been different in different traditions, but the Reality is Universal.

And yet the fact that some few *have* succeeded is a hope and an inspiration to us all. Or at least, it could be. What helps is the realization that the peak experience as defined by the psychologist Abraham Maslow is *universal*. It strikes quite without warning to any at the most outrageous times -- staring at the stars in the mountains, listening to the ocean waves at sunset, while jogging, just before sleep, in early childhood, over a crowded desk, walking alone down a deserted street in the wee hours before dawn, during childbirth -- the list of these magic moments is as extensive as is the human race itself. Suddenly the doors of perception burst open and the world is seen completely differently. In these rare, precious moments, a great "Aha!" surges through our souls; we recognize that the

Universe is, in fact, user-friendly, that life is good and beautiful, that maybe, just maybe, meaning exists here after all.

Since this experience is universal, there is great hope. Since it can strike anyone anywhere at any time, there is at least the hope that it can become systematic, that it can be regularly experienced, that all of us can share in it, not just the rare, fortunate or gifted.

This suggestion that peak experiences can become the ordinary experience of life may seem surprising. What is required here is to relax your guiding belief systems ever so slightly. I am not suggesting that you abandon any of your beliefs, but in order to derive benefit from this text on Ascension, it will be necessary to question -- ever so slightly! -- the belief that this quest is impossible or not for you. What, after all, do you have to lose by the thought that perhaps there might be a way of living your life that can generate a continual experience of joy, brilliance, creativity, health, and love? If you could have this, would you not want it?

There have been those throughout history who have described experiences of higher states of consciousness. These descriptions have frequently been so different as to make us feel that different realities were being described. When followers hold rigidly to the words of their Teachers without sharing the experience of conscious absorption in the Ascendant, then confusion is inevitable. This is the tragedy of knowledge: to break into small shards on the hard rocks of ignorance.

If both are fully developed human beings, there is no difference between the enlightenment of the Sufi Muslim and the absorption in God of the Christian saint. A fully realized Hindu in nirvikalpa samadhi is not living in a different state of consciousness from a perfectly adept Taoist established in Nirvana or a Zen Buddhist in permanent satori. We may appear different on the surface, our beliefs and language-concepts may be so widely at variance that we can hardly understand each other, but the essential inner Reality of consciousness is the same.

Even in the common, everyday waking state, we are much more similar than we are different. What will be most useful to our understanding of the nature of the Universe and of ourselves is the simple realization of how alike we all are.

We are all vessels of consciousness, of the light of the perfect Ascendant Source of all that is. It is not particularly difficult to realize this intellectually; the good news is that it is not particularly difficult to realize this Reality as a continual, twenty-four hours a day conscious experience. This is what is meant by "Praying without ceasing." (Praying without ceasing is most assuredly *not* trying to hypnotize the mind with continual verbal prayers and growing exhausted in the process!) The natural state of the human is to be established in continual experience of the Ascendant. This is the highest state of prayer even as it is the highest state of consciousness.

The simple truth is that it is far easier to be established in this state of permanent awareness of pure consciousness than it is not to be. It requires a tremendous amount of mental and therefore physical effort *not* to be enlightened! This wasted energy ages and ultimately kills the body; as we've already observed, this is exactly why we sleep so long at night and are so often sick and fearful during the days. We are struggling so hard to hold back the Infinite! It is actually much more difficult to deny inner awareness of the Ascendant than to experience it! Think about this. If it were possible this were true, would you not vastly prefer it to be so?

Fortunately, it is so; therefore all those who have proclaimed that it is difficult to meditate or pray to the One God must have missed this fundamental truth of the nature of life. If the Ascendant is present everywhere, including inside you, how can it possibly be difficult to know this? How can it possibly be difficult to experience this? Only shift the level of your appreciation of Reality and there you are.

Probably the belief in difficulty is the result of the perceived difficulty of abandoning belief systems that no longer serve us. We are told and have learned to believe that it is difficult to change our habits. We struggle, we moan, we complain when we decide that we "should" do something that is good for us or stop doing something that is bad for us, whatever the should might be: we *should* exercise more, we *should* stop smoking, we *should* stop drinking, we *should* stop overeating, we *should* stop abusing ourselves or our wives or our employees or our children.

This is going about life backwards. You don't have to beat a dog to keep it at the back door. You only have to feed it occasionally; the dog will never leave! Similarly, the mind does not like to be forced. But if new experience is introduced, the mind follows along, an obedient servant of your desire.

The mind has often been compared to a monkey, jumping from branch to branch. The proponents of concentration maintain the only way to still the mind is to beat it into compliance. Hard is this path and difficult to traverse even by the persevering. What is often missed is that the monkey is jumping from branch to branch *because it is seeking an ideal banana.* The mind moves because it is simply doing its job, seeking more and more enjoyment and experience; if we can provide it with the Ideal Experience of the Infinite Bliss of the Ascendant, it will naturally stay, perfectly still, enjoying that experience.

What happens in the growth of a human is this: the child is born essentially as a blank slate. Imprinting begins even in the womb. The behavior patterns and beliefs that we adopt are not consciously thought out -- we observe them and are subjected to them until we adopt them. What choice do we have? Our parents are as gods to us. It takes a rare soul to break through these deep-set habit patterns to look at life freshly, innocently, freely.

But why should it be difficult to know who we are? Can

it be that our habits are more deeply ingrained than we have yet imagined? Or has there been some kind of higher purpose, driving us ever deeper into matter, until the day we awaken in these human bodies in the twenty-first century on the planet we call Earth?

How we arrived at this point is a fascinating topic, one worth analyzing at some future time, but for now it is essentially irrelevant in helping answer the question, "How do we escape from here?" For this involves our immediate need.

THE DOOR OF EVERYTHING

The world seems a terribly frightening place. We humans are always at war with ourselves somewhere or other; the risks of human life are manifold and omnipresent. At any moment the body can be crushed, burned, frozen, exploded, destroyed; it can sicken, fail, die. We work all our lives to save up for retirement, then a recession comes or property values plummet or we make one bad investment or we go to war or some natural disaster strikes and our life's work is wasted. Or even if nothing of that sort happens, so often we don't adjust well to the changed pace and new demands of retirement and simply shrivel up and die. This life is always uncertain. Which of us has not had a close friend or relative leave us through that mysterious portal we call death? Where did they go? Why did they leave us? How many of us have been stricken by disfiguring accidents or horrible disease or addiction? This is a frightful, dangerous, terrible world. Or so it appears.

But there is another way of perceiving. Beneath the ever-changing tumult of the physical world lies a vast sea of non-changing peace. If we identify with the constantly rising and falling waves of the physical world, we will alternately enjoy and suffer and we will surely die. But fortunately it is possible -- and obviously highly desirable -- to identify more strongly with the ever-peaceful depths of the ocean of life than with the hurricane-torn surface of the sea of change.

Infinite stability, endless peace, permanent inner calmness is the result of this shift of our identification-awareness. This is not to say that a passive life is more desirable than an active one! The monk is no more likely to realize enlightenment than is the householder. The difference between a life of ignorance and a life of conscious realization of Inner Truth is not based on *anything* on the outside. Rigid vows are not required. Being permanently established in the Ascendant means that no activity, regardless how dynamic, can overshadow the Infinite silence and permanent peaceful stability of inner wakefulness. In this state, it becomes truly possible to be effective in life.

Before this change occurs, we are buffeted by the winds of life, blown here and there by the stresses of change, like a leaf before the gales of autumn. There is little peace, less stability. Our lives are lived in reaction to others' lives and actions, not truly creative, not established in the freedom and choice that living in the present instant provides. When we are enlightened, we do not *react*. We *act*. Free from self-destructive behavior patterns, beliefs and judgments, we act, creating flawlessly from the direct perception of the need of the moment. This is freedom; this is impeccably correct action. This is life in the present instant: the mind is no longer caught by regret for the past or worry about the future.

There is nothing to be gained by regretting our past experiences, choices and actions. The past is over; it does not exist here and now. By letting the past guide us, we are enslaved by our previous perceptions and beliefs.

Have you ever met a new person and immediately been attracted to her or him? Or have you ever felt repulsed by a new acquaintance, instantly upon your first glance, for no obvious reason? This is living life in the past. A face or body triggers a deep memory of another whom we loved or disliked; the new person is judged and filed away instantly, based on this ancient memory.

The enlightened have one inner response to everyone, and that is joy. It is always the same complete acceptance, manifesting unconditional love. This may or may not be perceived on the outside by another: there are no "laws of behavior" for the enlightened, there is no set pattern of living, dressing, diet, acting and no one set of beliefs. What is the same in all is the full awareness of the inner Infinite light; and, as handmaiden to that internal radiance, complete and perfect inner peace.

The Ascendant is Omnipresent, it is universal. It exists inside every human heart, inside every human mind, inside each and every grain of sand, inside every sun. It fills all of space and all of time with its wonderful radiance; there is no place it cannot be seen and fully known. Our role as self-conscious beings is to choose to look first for the light of the Ascendant.

The greatest secret of all is this: if we seek the Ascendant within our own hearts with all our spirit, not only our own selves but everyone else will automatically be healed. This is so because the seeming differences between us are not real. We are all one, quite literally. My salvation results in yours; I cannot be at peace and not infect you with peace. Some modern-day physicists have said that the fly walking on my living room wall also walks on Mars, also walks at the beginning and at the end of time. The fortunate truth is that this is literally much more accurate than they have perhaps themselves realized.

If I condemn my brother, who am I condemning? If I praise my sister, who am I praising? If we harbor dark thoughts inside, we can be absolutely sure of one thing: we will see darkness outside. If we are all light on the inside, it will be impossible to see anything but light outside. The Universe is our mirror: it is to us as we are to it.

This may seem nonsensical to some. Believing the world is flat does not make it flat. But what I am writing about is not based on belief; I am writing about direct, personal experience of the Source of all that is. The world reflects what we are, no more, no less. The world is as we are. We are our attention.

There is an ancient story which illustrates this point.

Once a young disciple wished to test the depth of his master's Self-realization. He had heard him say many times that the pure at heart can see nothing evil in the world and decided to find out if this were literally true for his master or was rather some sort of ideal belief.

This student led his Teacher down a deserted alleyway past a pile of garbage in which lay a rotting dog, victim of some disease of neglect. A more ugly sight the student could hardly imagine. As he led his master there, he said rather tremulously, "How disgusting, this rotting beast! You have told me all of life is filled with Truth and Beauty for those with the eyes to see it. But what is there of truth or beauty in this noisome carcass?"

His master turned his joy-saturated eyes toward him and laughingly replied, "Do you not see the little dog's sparkly white teeth? How they shine and dance in the moonlight! Are they not the most divinely formed pearls you have ever seen?"

In some versions of this story, the master's vision is so strong that the dog returns to vibrant life and health instantly.

Let us not confuse enlightenment with blindness. The fully enlightened alone can truly See. There are no preconceptions or judgments or previous experiences of life that can shroud the Reality of what *is*, right now. And what is, right now, is the perfection of the light of the Ascendant. This will become clearer as we progress; fortunately, it is not necessary to believe this in order to move ahead. It is in fact not necessary to believe anything written here to Ascend successfully. Ascension and evolution in general are not based on belief. Fortunately! Reality is not built on the foundation of human belief or compliance. It would be a rather odd world if Reality depended on our agreement!

The fully enlightened are not trapped into linear expression any more than they are trapped by linear perception. For example, the enlightened can appear (to all external appearances) to be filled with wrath --*if* the need of the environment is such. Sometimes, no medicine less strong than the voice of anger will suffice to move particularly dense students beyond their belief systems. But what never changes is the inner stability, the inner silence of the individual soul established in continual awareness of the Ascendant.

Not all enlightened individuals choose to become masters. Free will becomes more dominant, not less, after higher consciousness is stabilized. Many have been content to live lives of Silence, withdrawn from the frenetic movements of worldly life. But for some, Universal Mind decides that it will act in the world through a particular person; that one becomes a Teacher. How well known or how popular a Teacher becomes is not a measurement of inner Realization. The greatest may be content with a tiny grouping of students. Or they may not. It is all a grand Cosmic Play.

In the tradition of the enlightened, roughly half have chosen the path of the recluse and have withdrawn from the world, taking with them at most a handful of their closest followers; the other half have descended into the drama of Earth-life and founded new Teachings. It depends on the need of the time -- and upon the receptiveness of the people at that particular juncture in history. There is a profound intelligence at work in our world; every aspect of Universal Mind is being quite properly unfolded as it must be.

For example, the White, Red and Black Ishaya masters from the time of their founding by the Apostle John have been content to live a life of silence in the remotest regions of the Himalayas. They chose to save and preserve the Twenty-seven Techniques of Ascension for the modern world, keeping them hidden and secret until the dawn of the third millennium. More correctly stated: the Ishayas were instructed by Infinite

Intelligence to preserve Ascension in silence and seclusion until now.

And it is also true that now the Ishayas have been told and recognized the long-awaited time has come. That which has been long withheld is now being released: Ascension is to enter the world now. One of the Ishayas has been ordered to bring this Teaching into the world. One of their number, a Maharishi Black Ishaya of wisdom, compassion and power is founding this Teaching in the West for the benefit of all.

Fortunate are those who recognize the authority of this ancient Teaching and align with it: their lives will change in ways it is difficult even to conceive. Full enlightenment will dawn for them as their age-old habits of compromise and lack of full integrity fall away, and are replaced by the continual moment-by-moment experience of the One Unchanging at the center of their being. A complete life of bliss and Infinite Awareness will dawn for any who effortlessly treads the path of the Ishayas' Ascension.

And do you know what? Belief is not required. It is absolutely not required. Ascension is a series of mechanical techniques that require no belief to begin or practice. Isn't that nice?

VIII. THE ETERNAL CHOICE

The world is as you are.

I said earlier that it is our continual, moment-by-moment decision that keeps us turned away from the Infinite inner light and toward the incessant problems of relative life. This bears further explanation. We do not commonly feel that we are choosing over and over throughout the day *not* to be enlightened! And yet, even if we have some intellectual understanding of higher consciousness, still we typically put its realization far off in space or time, never Here and Now. Our initial decision was so far removed in time that Infinite Awareness may be only the haziest of memories, flickering rarely through us, playing with us in our dreams, dancing behind the sunbeams at the beach or magically but briefly surfacing when we gaze into our lover's eyes.

The blocks to Infinite Awareness can be removed by systematically undoing our previous decisions. One way to do this is by learning exactly what these decisions were. These ancient decisions have by now formed some extremely tenacious habit patterns that keep us turning away from the Ascendant, so one way to find the ultimate cause of our suffering is to look at some of the more obvious patterns that keep us in bondage. Then, by a circular reasoning, we can determine exactly what the root of all these false patterns is and thereby learn to turn from it in a permanent manner. If the root is abandoned, the manifestations of the root will surely die. In other words, it will not be necessary to struggle to change a habit pattern if the basis of the decision to continue with the habit has been eradicated from our minds.

One thought that causes a great deal of trouble to many is the belief that others are in some way responsible for the way we feel. We think that we are happy or unhappy because of the way others treat us. If others seem to be taking advantage of us, then that is sufficient cause for us to be unhappy. If a specific person does something to us that displeases us, we become upset at that person; if we perceive his or her actions as a threat to our security, we may take actions against him or her. Or we may withdraw into ourselves in an attempt to escape from him or her.

There are two problems with perceiving any one or any group as an enemy. First, the ones toward whom we turn our negative energy are not being helped to change by our response. They may in fact become more adamant in their offensive behavior. This is a curious but almost universal attitude of the human being. If we force them to behave as we desire, they may do so, but they will never do so with glad hearts or willing minds. "A man convinced against his will is a man of the same opinion still." All beings deeply resent being forced to do anything and will always, sooner or later, work against the desires of the dictator.

Secondly, even if we can force allegiance by our superior power or coerce a desired action by our negativity, the damage to ourselves from our action is certain. Like a ricocheting bullet, our actions fly back at us from every corner of the Universe. The worst result of this is that our awareness, instead of becom- ing more and more universal, more and more saturated with love and light, becomes more and more restricted and bound. By perceiving enemies in our world, we begin to slice off parts of our Universe, begin to label pieces of our cosmos as being in some way bad, evil or unworthy of our love.

As this process continues, our bodies begin to deteriorate. We may begin to walk stooped over, fatigued from carrying the weight of others' condemnation. Or we may distort our faces into habitual frowns or looks of disdain for the woefully inferior beings that inhabit this sick world. Or we may starve ourselves to the point of anorexia, or we may bloat ourselves to the size of a blimp in silent protest to the injustices of life.

Internally, the responses of this style of functioning are even more devastating, more lethal. As we condemn larger and ever larger populations to death and damnation, our hearts become more and more ossified; our health fails at an ever-increasing rate, resulting almost universally in an absurdly short life-span of a pitiful handful of seventy years.

There is another way. The immanence of the Kingdom of Heaven has been discussed and fervently believed in for thousands of years. But most have not understood or have ignored or have forgotten the fact that the Kingdom of Heaven comes from within. It grows first of all in the human heart. And one of the first steps in this process is to realize that all life is a part of us: every living being is our brother or sister; every living being is an extension of our perfect mind.

Everyone on the planet is a piece of the Ascendant. Everyone reflects the Infinite light. This necessarily means that everyone is equally worthy of our love. Others' actions, so horribly condemned by us when we believed that we can be hurt or victimized, begin to be seen as either expressions of love filtered through their individual nervous systems, or else as cries for our help. "Please demonstrate to me that you love me! Please show me that you will continue to care for me even if I fail chemistry or marry George or get fired! Please show me that you will still love me even if I hurt you."

The depth of the feeling of loneliness, of isolation, of fear combined with the extent of the feeling of victimization will determine the depth of the "negative" action employed by a soul seeking proof of love in a harsh Universe. In every case, it is a request for assistance. "I'm drowning here on Earth! Can't anyone help me? You say you love! You dare to say you love me! Prove it to me! I'll be bad, so very, very bad, because no one really truly loves me. You must prove it to me!"

This all means that there are only two kinds of actions on Earth, only two kinds of thoughts, only two kinds of feelings

-- those which are based in love and those which are based in fear -- fear of being alone, lost, unloved. Thus any "negative" actions or feelings or words only deserve our compassionate understanding, never our punishment or judgment. They are cries for help, for love. " 'Judgment is Mine,' says the Lord," is a statement of fact. Human beings have no business judging others. There is only one judgment, and that is that *all* are worthy of love and worthy of love and worthy of love. God only says one thing to the human, and that is, "Yes." It is our job here to attempt to master such a depth of unconditional love.

This may not be particularly easy to do at first. Our usual habit is to feel that the world is a more or less hostile place, in which we are frequently (or always) victims of circumstance, people or place. We are often prone to feel that we are being taken advantage of. We often feel that others are attempting to control or manipulate us. We often take this to the extreme and believe there are dark forces in the Universe who are attempting to destroy our souls. We feel that energy flows toward us to control us or to be a victim -- either of other people, or of Satan, or of a jealous, vengeful God, or perhaps of impartial and uncaring natural law.

VICTIM CONSCIOUSNESS

We commonly feel like this:

In this state, we feel that everyone is looking at us at all times, that we are the center stage of our Universe.

This is, of course, literally true, but not in the way we are feeling and

believing it to be in this state of Victim Consciousness. When enlightenment is stabilized, we *know* we are the center of the

Universe, (as is everyone else); we never feel like a victim. Our experience of others is now like this:

This is a state of continually giving love, joy, light, not taking. If the light bulb is turned on, it radiates light. There is no potential to be experiencing shadows, because there are no shadows anywhere that exist when we view life from this perspective. This is Seeing, this is the most effective way to exorcise the demons from our private Universe.

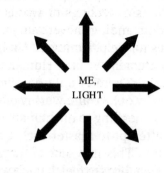

One characteristic of Victim Consciousness is the tendency to believe that life is being done *to* you, to feel that you are not the prime mover in the Universe, to feel that others have control over your feelings, moods and experiences. This belief frequently results in a desire to attack first, to strike out against others before they can strike out against you. This can occur physically -- a preemptive military strike is the most extreme example, but any action designed to hurt another qualifies as this kind of violence. This can also occur emotionally -- threats, pleading, anger are obvious examples.

If we believe that we can be hurt by another, it is only natural for us to believe that we can (and perhaps should!) attack first to save ourselves from the impending pain or destruction. The problem is that this doesn't save us from pain. In fact, this tends to increase pain, both in ourselves and, to the extent that our opponents also feel like victims, in others.

The alternative is to culture a state of consciousness in which it is impossible ever to feel betrayed, for it is impossible ever *to be* betrayed.

If we view ourselves as bodies, then we can certainly be betrayed. We can be damaged -- we can be cut, bruised, shot, torn. And we can obviously damage ourselves: we can give ourselves hypertension, heart disease, cancer, the com- mon cold; we can commit suicide; we can become insane.

But if we are spirit, it is impossible ever to betray or be betrayed. We cannot be damaged. We cannot be cut, bruised, shot, torn. We are, quite literally, invincible, indestructible, undying.

Some of us have realized this intellectually and others of us have attempted to live this state of consciousness by believing in it, by calling it grace or salvation or enlightenment and making a mood of living it: "Since I know logically that spirit is Omnipresent, I believe that I cannot be hurt in any way. My illness must be an illusion. I will therefore will it away."

Unfortunately, this rarely works. This is confusing the path to the goal for the goal itself. The only immediate advantage of this shift in perspective is the understanding that there is another way to view the Universe. Once this is realized, we naturally become eager to begin to develop this perception of life, for it means endless freedom, boundless joy, flawless love. As an experience, not just a belief.

THE PATHLESS PATH

What does the path to full awareness entail? First, the recognition that it is possible to be living more of life. It is not necessary to *believe* that it is possible to gain a permanent higher state of consciousness, but it is necessary to believe that it is possible to be better -- happier, healthier, more energetic, more intelligent. This is not necessary to make Ascension work (it will work anyway), but the "belief of possibility" is usually required for one to be bold enough to take the first step and begin the practice. Well begun is half done. Momentum will carry us forward after the first step, but to begin to break the past habit and belief patterns, this first step is required: we must recognize that change is not only possible but desirable.

Sincere willingness to change also helps. Some of us like to pretend we are willing to change but in fact are just deluding ourselves -- in reality, we would much rather hold onto the familiar old boundaries, even if those boundaries are killing us, than face the unknown future. We are so terrified of the unknown! And yet, we can never be terrified of the unknown, but only of the known. And the known that we fear is an illusion merely -- there is nothing to fear in Reality, only in the illusory coverings that we have imposed upon it.

Ascension provides a systematic series of procedures to move our awareness from Victim Consciousness to enlightenment. There are discrete, mechanical steps to be practiced until they are mastered. One purpose of this short text is to provide an intellectual understanding of the steps of growth to enlightenment. The actual mechanics of the experience can only be taught through personal instruction by qualified teachers. This is true primarily because it is not possible to verify the correctness of the practice without personal feedback.

Of the thousands I have personally instructed in meditation, every single one has succeeded in moving ahead in their lives. Those who move the most dramatically are those who are the most willing to change. Effort put toward finding the time to Ascend is amply rewarded. The practice is extremely easy, all but effortless, completely natural. And Ascension can be practiced with the eyes open or closed.

After the short daily periods of practice, it is certainly possible to accelerate growth. Exercise can be useful. Diet can be useful. Knowledge can be useful, but all the knowledge in the Universe will not serve you if you don't apply it. As I mentioned, that is why this is a short book. One more text cluttering up the shelves is a poor substitute for the direct experience of the Infinite Ascendant.

IX. UNIVERSAL ACCEPTANCE

When I accept others as they are, they change.
When I accept myself as I am, I change.
-- Carl Rogers

Ascension is Universal -- those of any religious background can and do learn this practice. The Teachers of Ascension uphold all religious traditions and honor all religious leaders, past and present. Any and all attempts to grow toward the Ascendant are beneficial; any and all past attempts have contributed greatly to human life. We honor all and condemn none, for we know that everyone in deepest essence is a spark of the Divine Flame. The external differences that are so apparent in the Earth-life are quite superficial compared to the Infinite, never-changing light that underlies and permeates all of creation. This inner light accepts all, flatters none, condemns none. How could it? It is the essential Reality of everyone, of everything, everywhere, always.

This attitude of universal acceptance can be artificially cultured -- it is, after all, only a mental habit that leads us to condemn others. Any habit can be changed. If it is possible to think with judgment about ourselves and others, it is certainly possible (and definitely easier) to think without judgment, with perfect acceptance of ourselves and everyone else.

How often have we condemned others? How often do we berate ourselves for some of our habits that we have judged unworthy? But there is a part of us that will continue to strengthen our "bad" habits, to match our will step-by-step, energy level by energy level, for there is a part of our soul that insists we love ourselves regardless of our condemned habits. There is a point deep inside each of us that consists of perfect ruthlessness, of absolute lack of pity. Our higher Self is committed to our learning all that it is necessary to learn. We will do anything required to our lower selves in order to learn.

Anything. Crippling disease. Early death. Misshapen bodies. Hideously destructive habits. Anything at all. And all for growth.

Similarly for our attitude toward others. Others wish to be loved just as they are. They don't wish to change to suit our desires: why should they? Does the Sun fail to shine for them too? Has the oxygen ceased to nourish their cells? If the Universe continues to accept and love them just as they are, why are we any less gracious?

This may be one of the harder principles to grasp, for we have all devoted vast quantities of our energy to support our beliefs that some standards of behavior are better than others. We have a deep propensity to think like herd animals -- actions are "all right" as long as others do them or accept them. Why is there a drug problem in this country? One reason is that our peers' opinions and feelings are much more important than impersonal authority figures, even when the authority figures have no end to the logic and science backing up their opinions.

Is there, then, no universal standard of behavior? From the standpoint of the Ascendant, no one has ever left or ever will leave (or even can leave) Infinite Consciousness. But from the perspective of beings who have forgotten everything of the Ascendant -- even the fact of its existence -- it is obvious that some actions will keep us from remembering who we are longer than will others. And certain acts will propel us in the direction of removing the self-imposed blocks to experience of the Ascendant, whereas others will increase the obstructions.

Certain foods nourish the body more than others. Certain kinds of exercise are more useful than others. Certain ways of thinking are beneficial, others are not. Certain beliefs are useful for our evolution, some are not. Certain habits and actions speed our progress; others hinder our growth and the growth of others. Such actions are not "sins," we are not punished for slowing our evolution or others' evolution, but we do experience less happiness when we hinder growth, and in this sense we suffer and would be happier by choosing again to remake those particular choices which are causing pain.

This is the application of the law of cause and effect in the human sphere -- the law of karma as it was known in the East, the law of retribution as it was called by Emerson and others in the West, the fundamental creed of every religion, the Golden Rule which was perhaps best expressed in Galilee nearly two thousand years ago -- "Do unto others as you would have them do unto you. " And, "As you sow, so shall you reap." If we plant seeds of fear, discord and disharmony, we will certainly harvest a crop of unhappiness. If we plant the seeds of love, the Invincible Forces of Nature will respond by bringing an abundant harvest of joy and love into our world.

This is why it is important to treat others as we wish to be treated. Not because we can permanently injure them or ourselves -- since we are all eternal impulses of life, that is simply impossible. Bodies can and will be lost, souls never. But we can slow others' return to their Source -- or we can hasten it. And as we slow or hasten others' return, our return will be slowed or hastened, for the others in our Universe are, in the final analysis, only extensions of ourselves.

If we are devoted to material gains or material possessions, our focus is on that which will pass away. If our energy goes to these mutable things and not to that which never changes, our life will inevitably meet with decay and death. If, on the other hand, we devote our existence to that which never changes, our life will respond by becoming more and more imbued with the dynamic and invaluable qualities of the Ascendant.

From the standpoint of Eternity, what difference does it make if it takes an immortal impulse of Eternal Life a day or a year or a hundred million years to remember it is an immortal impulse of Eternal Life? How much difference to Infinity any number, however large? There is none. But from the standpoint of the forgetful impulse, a day does indeed seem different from a hundred million years! It is all a matter of perspective.

When we are young, if the arm of our prized doll breaks, we experience terrible pain and may roll on the floor in tears. Our wise and loving mother, drying our tears, repairs the arm or buys us a new and better doll or in some other way expands the horizon of our experience. From the point of view of the mature adult, the child's problems are generally easy to solve. Only adults who are still themselves emotionally children have trouble with these situations.

Many may find taking this one step further difficult, but it is certainly valuable. When our Universe is shaken to its core by the death of a loved one or by a terrible debilitating illness or by another of the innumerable vicissitudes of Earth-life, it is only human to shake our fist at the Creator, to feel anger, pain, suffering. It is only human, but it is not Divine.

Not only is it not necessary to suffer in this human life, it is never necessary or even useful to struggle against the natural current of our lives. We may not always understand or remember where we are going, we may not always understand or remember why we experience our lives as we do, but this does not mean that we will never understand or remember. Sometimes a little more patience is all that is required; sometimes a slightly different way of looking at our lives or world is all that is necessary. And sometimes we need to demonstrate to ourselves that we really are, after all, the ones who created our world exactly as it is.

This concept may seem quite startling upon first contact. We normally think that we are thrust, all unwilling, into a Universe that we most certainly did *not* create. We feel our parents owe us a living for making us. After all, we didn't ask to be born, did we?

From this initially hostile world, we are supposed to make something out of our lives -- we are supposed to succeed, progress, prosper, be responsible adults and citizens.

Impersonal fate (or a wrathful God) may have dealt us a hard hand -- we may have damaged bodies or our external circumstances may have been extremely hard from birth. We may have been born addicted or diseased; we may have been born with a weak heart or liver. In these cases, we are supposed to make the best of our lives and world -- to persevere and succeed in spite of our hardships. We believe in so many "shoulds" and "should nots" here on Earth!

I do not mean to imply that it is wrong to strive for greatness. I do mean to imply that it is wrong to blame others for our physical, mental, emotional or environmental reality. This is not wrong in the sense of being damaging, it is wrong in the sense of being a waste of time in that it supports a faulty and limiting belief system that does not serve us.

If people from former ages could be magically transported to the present, they would doubtless consider many of our modern conveniences which we take for granted -- TVs, cars, lights, telephones, airplanes -- to be miraculous, either divine or satanic. It is a common human response to the unknown to throw up our hands and invoke some sort of mysterious supernatural agency. When we don't understand something, we say, "It must be God's will," or "It's just fate," or "It's all luck," or "Satan did it." We have a convenient label for what we don't understand so that we don't have to think about it. *Why did my best friend have to be killed in his private plane when he was so happy and brilliant and successful? Why did my father have to die in my arms when I was fourteen? Why was my son born blind? Why is my boss so mean? Why did my wife have terminal cancer? Why is life so meaningless? Why is God so cruel? Why, God, why?*

It is true that none of us is ever likely to know everything that there is to know. Who would want to? I personally don't care how many grains of sand there are in the Sahara. Do you? But it is quite possible to know anything at all. If our philosophy of life or our belief system is consistently running into a brick wall where there is no recourse but to leave a vast amount of experience unexplained or explained only by invoking God's will or impersonal fate -- then we would be wise to ask ourselves if perhaps our system of thought is substituting belief for direct understanding. If we are told to "accept on faith" because "certain things are not open to human understanding" -- watch out! We can spend our entire lifetime in that intellectual cul-de-sac, and when it is over, we will be right back where we were in the beginning -- trying to understand *why* the Universe is as it is.

Please don't accept anything the Ishayas teach on faith! Blindly accepting another's philosophy is the surest path to remaining solidly in Victim Consciousness. Make your own experiment with life: study your mind and experience, take nothing for granted, from the most ordinary to the most miraculous. There only lies progress.

This is why Ascension is based on direct experience. There is no necessity for believing anything about it. Try it for yourself. As your beliefs and habits begin to shift with your changing experience of life, inquire more and more deeply exactly what is true and what is not, more and more deeply what is Real and what is not. Thus only freedom comes.

A large part of assuming the mastery of our own lives consists in ceasing to put anyone else on a pedestal of authority. It is also difficult or impossible to assume mastery over our own lives if we blame others or circumstances "beyond our control" for the way our lives are going. It is impossible to be free if we maintain the mental chains of past or present condemnation or slavish devotion. Realize this now, and you have made a huge step forward toward your immediate liberation. Realize this now and you have discovered one of the fundamental secrets of human life -- there is no one to blame, no one to thank, no one but ourselves.

The next step may prove equally difficult to grasp on first consideration but is equally important and is even more liberating from past self-destructive beliefs, judgments and habit patterns. It is this: each of our lives, right now, is perfect. Everything and everyone in our Universe is there for a good reason -- they are there to help us recognize our True Nature. This is always so, no exceptions, ever. Each and every moment is impeccable, unblemished, flawless in every way because it is saturated with the Infinite light of the Ascendant.

This concept is revolutionary only because we are in the habit of judging everyone, everything, every thought, every feeling and every experience as being either "good" or "bad." Some people we like, others we detest. Some emotions are positive, others are negative. Some experiences are wonderful, others are horrible. And so on. We believe in a world of duality -- of hot and cold, of wet and dry, of pleasure and pain.

GOOD ASCENDANT VS. BAD ASCENDANT

Let's consider the alternative we face at its most basic. There are really only two possibilities -- either the Ascendant is good or the Ascendant is bad. Isn't this so? If the Ascendant is bad, then a meaningless or at least a painful Universe is perfectly logical and consistent. But if the Ascendant is bad, why should the Universe be logical or consistent? So, if the Ascendant is bad, the Universe would most likely be fundamentally chaotic. Our Universe does, in fact, appear quite chaotic from day to day, but only in isolated instances. Basically, there can be no question that profound order is found permeating every particle of creation: this fundamental order holds the atoms together in quite consistent and uniform ways in your sun, in your dog, in your body. What kind of an Ascendant would establish as fundament perfect, flawless, universal order?

The Ascendant could be bad and so perverse that perfect order underlies a surface chaos everywhere. This could be a definition of hell: perfect order hides just beneath the surface, but all that is ever experienced is dark, painful, insane.

Most people are quite mad at their idea of the Ascendant, their personal idea of God. Many who profess great faith are nevertheless, deep inside, enraged that they have been so deeply hurt and betrayed. This is one of the roots of Victim Consciousness -- instead of blaming our parents or our husbands or our environment or our personal history, we blame the Supreme Being as the ultimate cause of our misery. Some, being secretly angry, are also terrified that their God will punish them for their disobedience or for their sinful, rebellious nature against the laws of chaos imposed upon them by their God or for their being secretly angry at their God.

If the Ascendant is truly bad, these people and others similar to them have every right to be terrified of their vengeful, spiteful God. Certainly such a Being would have no qualms about breathing life into uncountable trillions of beings, setting them to impossible tasks, slowly and painfully killing them all, and then relegating them all either to oblivion or to Eternal Damnation. If such a God existed, we would all -- or almost all -- be in serious trouble indeed: which of us has not broken most if not all of the many laws of the Earth-life?

This kind of God is not just bad, he is most certainly insane as well. What sane being would create life only to destroy it? Or create Immortal Life only to eternally punish it? These concepts are so incredibly absurd, so patently ridiculous, the only truly amazing thing about them is that so many human beings have so fervently expressed and defended them for so many centuries.

Let us consider the alternative. If the Ascendant is good, how is it possible that there can be pain or suffering in the world? Many have said that the Ascendant is good, but there are other powerful forces which are not. These other forces oppose the Ascendant's will mightily and continually. Some say that the Ascendant created only good, but some creatures decided to try to be greater than the Ascendant and rebelled in a mighty war that greatly diminished the Universe and almost destroyed creation itself. The arguments defending the Ascendant's lack of Omniscient foresight or strangely limited Omnipotence are truly fascinating, but all boil down to a God that is good, but not quite perfect. Or at least not quite all-intelligent or all-powerful.

A God that is not quite perfect is a bad God. What seems to be happening is that people who simply can't understand how the Universe can be flawed have to find a cause for the flaws. This is projection in its purest sense. I find the Universe flawed, therefore its Maker must be flawed -- or must be opposed by a nearly equally powerful and flawed being, which means the same thing in other words. For if there can be a second being who is almost but not quite as wise as God and almost but not quite as powerful as God and almost but not quite as good as God, there must be somewhere in the Universe where God is not. If God is not Omniscient, not Omnipotent, not Omnipresent, not particularly loving, kind or forgiving, He hardly sounds anything like God. But He does sound much like our own projected worst fear. If we worship or attempt to appease such a God, we are worshipping or attempting to appease our own fear, our own dark natures. Therefore: *we are worshipping our own egos!*

A nearly Omnipotent but wrathful being, capable of crushing us all like noxious insects, more than willing to condemn us to an unending lifetime of pain and torture if we don't keep his many rules -- why would we want to believe in such a Being? One reason might be to force us to behave rightly -- for a part of us frequently believes that if we don't make ourselves do the right thing, we will respond by becoming wild, selfish, deranged, and soon damage ourselves and others. And if we don't even trust ourselves to "be good," how can we even dream of trusting others? As a tool for forcing compliance from ourselves and others, then, a bad, mad God becomes a worthy ally.

The trouble with consciously or unconsciously repressing Truth for the sake of forcing conformity is that it will, sooner or later, breed rebellion. And the more forcefully we attempt to crush the revolt, the more strength the revolution will gain. Our church will splinter as ever larger groups of humanity are condemned to Eternal hellfire, for the definition of exactly what it is that God requires will have to be more and ever more rigidly drawn. When we die, we will be careful to be buried in the graveyard next to *our* church -- we wouldn't want even our dead and rotting carcass to be associated with those heathens and sinners who are certainly going to roast in the fires of hell from Eternity to Eternity.

Peace be to such foolishness! The Ascendant Truth is equally in all or in none.

If the Ascendant is truly all good, all powerful, present everywhere, then the only other alternative is to question our previous perceptions and our conclusions based on those perceptions. When you eliminate the impossible, what remains, however improbable it might seem, must be the truth. We have seen what happens when we project our pain and suffering outward -- God becomes cruel, impotent, bad, insane, or at the least, indifferent. But what if our projections are false? Suppose, for the sake of argument, that the Ascendant truly is all good, all powerful, present everywhere, perfectly loving and caring for each and every one of His/Her creations. Let us take a good Ascendant as our starting point and see what kind of a Universe results from this premise.

If the Ascendant is truly all good, then how can there be pain or suffering of any kind? If the Ascendant is truly all love, how could any level of creation suffer? And if the Ascendant does not permit or condone suffering and some of creation suffers anyway, does this not prove that there is a second, malefic will in Creation, opposing the will of the Ascendant?

There is another possibility. This is an ancient idea, but it has fallen out of vogue in most of the world due to lack of understanding of how to make it anything other than a particularly fascinating thought. We *can* take as premise the fact that the Ascendant is Omnipresent, perfectly good and Omnipotent *if we question our conclusions and perceptions that suffering and evil exist.* When we awaken from a dream, what of the dream characters? What of the dream pains, the dream beliefs? They vanish as if they had never been.

TWO KINDS OF EVIL

There are two kinds of evil, or so we often believe -- that which results in eventual good, and that which is purely destructive with no positive effects. The second kind is the only significant challenge to the understanding of the all-good nature of the Ascendant, for the first kind, the kind that results eventually in good, must simply *be* good, and only our limited understanding of cause and effect makes us interpret it differently. Someone could declare it bad that buds die. But wait just the shortest of moments -- soon a flower emerges. Who now decries the loss of the bud? So this first kind of evil is simply misinterpreted good, due solely to the limited range of our senses and understanding.

The fortunate truth is that the second kind of evil, the kind that is purely evil with no good effects, is strictly a mental fabrication of the most bizarre sort. The simple reality is that all things work together for good always. It is only our perspective that is limited, it is only our eyes that have learned to see wrongly. This is a wonderful thought, even if it can be entertained for only an instant. If all evil works eventually for good, then what is evil? It must be a tool of the Ascendant! The caterpillar dies; from one perspective, this is bad, but look what happens as the result: a butterfly is born! Is the death of the caterpillar evil? If we were overly attached to the caterpillar, its death might seem evil to us, horrifying, terrible. But look at the beauty that results.

I'm sure you can easily think of counter-examples of this theory, thousands of times in the history of your world and your life when terrible things happened that resulted in no good. Some of you may have already abandoned this work, muttering that it is another form of mysticism or something equally useless to practical life. Or perhaps it has already deeply offended your religious sensibilities, so painfully acquired, and you are still reading only to find further proofs and demonstrations that this Teaching is invalid, Satanic or in some other way damaging. And perhaps some of you who are still reading, a deep hunger in your hearts, are continuing only with the gravest of reservations. So much of human experience seems pointless, filled with pain. We feel we have been betrayed so often before. What if the Ishayas' Ascension Techniques are only another disappointment? Surely it's better not to become involved. Surely it's better to be safe than be hurt again.

I agree that suffering is the *apparent* truth. I agree that this truth appears quite incontrovertible, that evil, pain and agony seem the perpetual handmaidens of our short lives. But I would ask you to consider for a moment what it would mean if you could see the alternative. What would it mean if life were not meant for suffering? What if life is in reality meant for all joy, love, progress, happiness?

There is a marvelous older movie, perhaps you have seen it, called, "It's a Wonderful Life." The protagonist, Jimmy Stewart, agonizing over the uselessness of his existence, is shown what the world would have become had he never lived. Everything of his town, everything of the lives of his family and friends was much worse off without his being there. The point was wonderful: from our human perspective, it is exceedingly difficult to evaluate the effect we are having on the Universe.

We could take this one step further, for the absence of anyone's life is simply impossible: all things are part of the grand Cosmic Design. That this does not often appear to be so does not change the fact that it is so. It is still true that Reality is not now and never will be democratic.

A NEW WAY OF LIVING

Consider what the requirements for growth of happiness and health are. If our old world-view is outmoded, not giving us everything we desire, if we are sick or not filled with continual joy of life, it is necessary to introduce a new way of living, a new way of perceiving, a new level of consciousness into our lives. To do this, we must allow our old, cherished beliefs to change. For it is exactly our beliefs that structure our perceptions and our world. It is not probable that peaches will grow on apple trees. If we have grown discontented with apples and desire peaches, we must plant a different kind of tree. If there are areas of our life in which we are discontented, in which we are not living in complete fulfillment, perfect peace, unbounded joy, and if we wish to change these areas, it is necessary to adopt a different way of looking at our lives and our world.

When we look with condemnation on ourselves or others, we contribute to a lowering of the vibratory rate of the Universe. This does not mean that we should attempt to repress our negative feelings if we have them! Repression of negativity is one of the major causes of the breakdown of our mental, emotional and physical health. It does us no good to have negative feelings about someone or something and then force ourselves to ignore them. They will have their effects anyway. And the effects will be stronger the more energy we feed them through repression. But it is possible to culture a state of consciousness in which we look with divine compassion on the world always. Instead of looking out and seeing sin everywhere, we look out and see all people trying to do the best they can.

This is the perception of the enlightened -- all people are doing the best they can, everywhere, always. No exceptions. We might say that one person's best may be another's worst -- but this is comparison, judgment, condemnation, not love and forgiveness. It is better for our own peace of mind to have only one conclusion about the world, that everyone is doing absolutely the best he or she can at all times. This is the immediate and practical derivative of the conclusion that the Ascendant is all Good, that the Ascendant is all Love, present everywhere, all-knowing.

Another way to say this is to say: "At all times, there is only good." What a relief to a tired mind to think such a simple thought! Entertaining this one thought challenges us to see the good in that which the surface mind has judged to be bad or unworthy. Entertaining this one thought propels us deeper and deeper into the growth of our individual consciousness. Entertaining this one thought inspires us to learn of the good in all things.

X. ENLIGHTENMENT

There is no distance between you and your Good.

What exactly is enlightenment? Everyone has been talking about it for years, but what is it? Is it different from the Salvation of the Christian tradition? Is it the same for Buddhists, Hindus, Taoists, Sufis, Muslims, Christians, agnostics, atheists? What exactly is the Voice for God? Can anyone experience it? Can there be modern prophets and sages, or were they an historical phenomenon only, never found in the modern world? Or did they ever exist at all? Was their supposed existence only historical aggrandizement? Are miracles real, or are they fantasy merely?

Do these questions deeply move you? If they seem impractical to you, of little relevance to your life and your world, they probably don't interest you much. If this is so for you, what does fascinate you? What interests a modern human being? Are we all content with the quality of our lives? Do we, any of us, care what is the possible range of human experience? Or are we too interested in our financial and social standing to care about anything else? What if expansion of consciousness resulted in greater success in every area of our concern? And what if it were truly possible to do anything we desired, anything at all? Would we be interested then?

For some of us, it may be that we were once interested, but then we stumbled across a teacher or a teaching or a minister or a church or a science and are now completely content with receiving answers from others, and rarely or never seek for our own inner truth. Or it may be that we despaired of ever finding answers and abandoned our quest.

Another way to find no answer is to try a little of everything available and deeply experience nothing. We occasionally have such people come and learn some of the Ishaya Techniques. These have a habit of trying everything they find, thrashing about wildly, seeking everywhere for truth, finding it nowhere. This grab-bag approach to enlightenment is never successful. Only by diving deep into one's own heart can progress ever be made. Only by seeking within are answers ever found. Adopting someone else's belief system is no answer. Blindly following yet one more teacher or teaching is ultimately pointless. The True Teacher will always point the finger of understanding back at the heart of the seeker. There only is progress possible. The True Teacher always seeks independence in his/her followers, never slavish devotion. Growth comes from the inside out. Always. Always.

Within each of us lies a treasure house of undiscovered wealth. Beauty greater than human eyes have ever beheld is hidden inside our hearts; wisdom greater than human minds have ever known is cached within the secret jewelled chamber within our breasts. Safety, security, freedom from fear of every kind lie there, as do fulfillment of every desire, calmness from every storm, a loving hand to dry every tear, a peaceful balm to soothe every hurt.

What can be done to liberate our hidden genius? Even modern psychology has declared that the average person uses a frighteningly small percentage of the mental potential available -- most agree that only 5% to 10% of our human capacity is employed by the average adult. What a tragic waste of life that so much of our inner mind is never used, lies forever untapped, unappreciated, unknown!

Lying inside each of us is a magnificent reservoir of creativity and brilliance. It is not difficult to learn how to tap this inner repository. What stands in the way is just habit. It is habit that restricts the use of our minds; it is habit that keeps us believing in a limited life of ups and downs, of pleasure and pain, of success and failure. Any habit can be broken or retrained. If it is our beliefs that keep the mind chained to a tiny fraction of its full potential, these beliefs can be changed.

Ascension is a systematic procedure for re-educating

the mind to free itself from judgment and condemnation. This is a completely automatic process; once begun it continues much by itself. The mind is similar to a phonograph record -- there are grooves in our brains, neuronal circuits, formed by repeated experiences and thoughts. The more we perform a specific action or have a specific thought, the more deeply the grooves are cut into our brains. This is something of a curse as far as life-damaging habits are concerned, but it is of course a great blessing as well: life would be extremely impractical if we had to try to remember how to walk every time we took a step, for example.

It is possible to retrain the mind so that the deepest grooves are those that lead to expansion of consciousness, to liberation. Every technique of concentration attempts to do this by force; every psychologist and psychiatrist is attempting, however blindly, to undo the deepest patterned behaviors and replace them with a greater degree of holistic autonomy; every good religious leader hopes to accomplish a lessening of the negative behavior patterns of his followers by an introduction of higher spiritual power.

We honor and respect all useful approaches to the transformation of human awareness from the field of problems to the field of all solutions, the Source of all that is. From our experience, it is clear that it is not difficult to change life -- it is, in fact, perfectly easy.

Let me give you an example. If you adore German Chocolate Cake -- and assuming you don't feel you are overweight, are not dieting, have no physical problems or mental compunctions about eating sugar or fat, no reasons of any kind not to enjoy German Chocolate cake -- and you are hungry and someone offers you a piece, will it be difficult to take it and eat it and enjoy it? But what will happen if you feel that you are overweight, are dieting, are concerned about your blood sugar and cholesterol, you just finished a huge seven-course meal, you're counting your pennies and it costs $7.50 a slice? If you do decide to eat it, will you enjoy it much?

How often do we do exactly this to ourselves? We invest a vast amount of our emotional, spiritual and intellectual strength into the fulfillment of a desire, all the while undermining our efforts with a continual chorus of counter-doubts and desires. Some of these are often so habitual or so well hidden that we don't even realize what we are doing to ourselves until it is too late.

The human mind is a fascinating tool. It is sufficiently complex to do anything, anything at all. The number of possible combinations and permutations of the neurons in the human brain is larger than the number of atoms in the entire Universe. This is a truly amazing, nearly infinitely complex machine, capable of realizing any truth, of having any experience. The human brain is sufficiently subtle that it can even experience consciousness itself, the most abstract essence of everything.

If this remarkable machine can act in a completely unified manner, the power of its thought force is strong enough to do anything. This is what Christ was speaking of when he declared that if your faith is like a grain of mustard seed, you can move mountains. The power of the perfectly concentrated mind is quite literally unlimited.

But the power of the divided mind is weak, ineffectual. If we desire a thing, the trick to accomplishing the desire is not to undermine the desire with a myriad of counter-desires. This, again, is a habit. The mind can be trained to think one-pointedly, or it can continue to think as most human minds think, in conflict and diversity. Ascension's simple suggestion is that this process of re-training is not only effortless but easy, completely natural and extremely quick.

Part of the secret is to charm the mind during every phase of this transformation. The mind is always greedy for more experience, more love, more peace, more stimulation, more knowledge -- always *more*. The fortunate fact is that the field of most already lies within -- the mind just needs to learn how to take the correct angle, then the entire process is perfectly automatic. Indeed, it will be impossible to stop the new grooves in the brain from deepening and intensifying until the older grooves are overshadowed and eventually erased.

The reason for this is that the natural state of human consciousness *is* enlightenment! The human mind would rather function with flawless and one-pointed desiring than in any other way. It would rather permanently experience its most expanded state than any more limited quality of its being. This requires only the slightest of modifications in the way it has been taught to view itself and its world; this miraculous transformation occurs automatically.

Primarily, it is guilt and fear that keep the mind caught in the belief that it is not enlightened. This may not be immediately obvious, but a careful and honest scrutiny of your own mind will reveal that there are usually only two kinds of thoughts -- those that are based in love and are unifying and those that are based in fear and are dividing. If you closely watch your mind for even five minutes, you will probably be quite astounded by the myriad of pointless and mutually contradictory thoughts and desires you experience. We have in our possession the most incredible machine in the Universe, capable of experiencing any reality, competent to discover any truth, equipped to accomplish any desire. What is typically being done with this magnificent machine? The standard mode of operation is to switch between mutually contradictory thoughts and desires dozens of times every minute! If the mind were a radio receiver, it would be as if it were being switched between channels every second or so -- it would make for a noisy, unpleasant reception, hard to follow. It would, in fact, be so hard to follow that you would feel exhausted after trying to listen to it for a few hours; you would feel forced to turn it off and just listen to nothing at all for a time.

This is our experience in the waking state. The mind *is*

a receiver of perceptions, images and thoughts; they file through it in unending succession until it becomes so exhausted it has to shut down to restore its badly depleted molecular resources and subtle powers. Hence we sleep.

The mind is not just a receiver of sensory information. It is sufficiently subtle to connect directly to the mindstuff that is the fundamental constituent of the Universe -- the mind is a machine that connects you, the individual, to the Universal Source of everything, to the Ascendant. When the mind is one-pointed, when its energies are concentrated as one, it is capable of not only experiencing the Ascendant but of transmitting its desires into the Ascendant.

THE ASCENDANT

When we perceive the external world, we are looking at our definitions of forms and objects, but not the underlying Unified Field in which they appear. Similarly, in our inner world, feelings and thoughts clutter our awareness, but the awareness of awareness itself is never known. The Ascendant is the space in which things exist; it is the essence out of which everything is made: thoughts, feelings, computers, my aunt Daisy.

This is not a void as some have claimed, this is not an empty or negative reality. Rather, the Ascendant is a positive state of fullness, of Infinite potential energy out of which everything comes. Since the Ascendant underlies and permeates everything in creation, it is called Omnipresent. Everything comes from it and exists only because of it. Nothing can or does exist in isolation. Everything is composed of the Ascendant, continually flowing in and out of manifestation.

The Ascendant cannot be measured or defined. We can assign a name to it, like Infinite or Unbounded or Absolute, but these still imply it is *something*. Any name for the Ascendant or belief about the Ascendant is *not* the experience of the

Ascendant. It is only when we abandon our insistence on attempting to limit the Unlimited by assigning waking state concepts to it that the Infinite light of the Primal World dawns within. Freed from mental fabrications about the nature of Reality, awareness is experienced as Absolute and identical with everything that is.

The Ascendant is without prior cause, it is its own cause; it is ever-the-same, unchanging. Like water, it is not altered regardless how much dirt is added to it: only the clarity of it is shrouded while its essential nature remains the same. The Ascendant is perfect stability -- it is the Ground of all grounds. There is no experience of duality in the Ascendant, there is no difference between the self and the Self. There is no separation. Like a peak experience while painting, writing or composing music, there is no subject-object duality. There is no thought in the Ascendant, there is no feeling, there is nothing other than Silence, Eternal, self-sufficient.

The Ascendant is the Ultimate Reality from which everything has come and in which everything continues to exist forever. To experience this as our True Nature *is* enlightenment; to remain ignorant of this means remaining caught by the boundaries of illusion, life after life, caught on the wheel of samsara, of cyclic change. Through Ascending, the Ascendant is experienced as our own essential nature, as awareness of awareness itself, as pure, Unlimited consciousness. This is the experience of Infinite Freedom. This is liberation from the boundaries of the ego. Since the Ascendant is the Source of everything, recognizing that *"I am That"* means that I recognize that I am all-pervasive. This is the state of Is-ness, free from any and every duality, freed from the sense of My-ness or even Am-ness. The Ascendant simply *is*. And *That* I am.

Even though the experience of the Ascendant is impossible to define in words, it *is* a real experience. In fact, the experience of the Ascendant is *more* real than any waking state experience. The experience of the Unbounded is infinitely abstract and yet infinitely concrete. Having once tasted this clearly, life cannot remain the same. There is no previous behavior pattern, habit, judgment or belief that can withstand the force of Unbounded Awareness, for the Ascendant is the root of *everything*.

When the mind is experiencing the silence of the Ascendant, there is no motion of thought. Like a perfectly still pond untouched by wind, there are no waves, no ripples, no motion of any kind when the mind is opened to the experience of the Ascendant. This state *is* measurable by the electroencephalograph: coherence of brain waves is the objective measurement of the subjective experience of Ascending.

The mind consumes vastly less energy when it floats in the Ascendant; because of this, the body settles down to its deepest possible state of rest. In the perfect state of Infinite silence, there is no necessity for breath: the individual retains life by recognizing that he or she is part of Universal Life, in no way different or separate from Eternal existence. In other words, life continues because life is the essence of the Ascendant. In this state, no decay is possible, no illness, no death, no suffering, no pain.

DREAMING

One of the most fascinating facts about the Ascendant is that any impulse of energy that moves there immediately reacts within it to manifest form. Our dreams at night imperfectly react with the Ascendant to produce visions of unlikely events of anything and everything. Because we are not usually very conscious while sleeping, we have little control of our mind-machine interacting with the Ascendant. Therefore, it rarely feels as if we are guiding our dreams. This can be changed by practice. There are potentially great gains to be had from studying dreams.

Since the Ascendant is the repository of Infinite Intelligence, and since many of our inhibitions about contacting the Ascendant are relaxed while we are sleeping, a high degree of subtle order underlies our dreams. Understanding what they are telling us, learning what messages are coming to us from our higher Self in the field of dreams makes a fascinating field of study. Mastering the pure creativity of dreams can open the door to mastering the ability to create anything desired.

Dreaming was sacred in many ancient civilizations. It was believed that dreams opened us to the abode of celestial forces; therefore no intelligent person ignored the advice gained from the supernatural realms entered in dreams. Some highly advanced societies built temples where individuals would go to dream and gain the counsel of the gods -- for example, ancient Egypt and Greece had many hundreds of such. Even today, certain aborigines hold that the most important state of consciousness is dreaming. A common feature of this belief is that our waking state world is in fact being dreamed by Someone Else. This understanding was also found in ancient India: Narayana (Vishnu) sleeps on the serpent Sesha (the repository of all previous Universes) on the Cosmic Ocean (the Ascendant), His dreams create Universes of name and form, one of which we happen to inhabit.

This mirrors truth: the waking state of consciousness is not Absolute. Our experience of life is not solid or unchanging, but is produced by our beliefs and judgments. If we wish, we can change our minds; this necessarily gives us a different perspective on life. Suffering is not necessary in waking anymore than it is in dreaming -- we can change our perceptions and experiences by changing our beliefs. We do not have to remain bound to our spatial, temporal, cultural, familial, or past interpretations of the world. And yet for most, particularly those who are not evolving to higher levels of consciousness, the dictates of rationality and empirical reasoning *appear* Absolute: it is difficult if not impossible to rewrite the lifelong dream that is our waking state drama.

But for everyone, the dreaming state is free of all restrictions, which is exactly why so many have such a hard time understanding the symbols hiding in dreams. Every dream can serve as a source of healing or insight; dreaming integrates our experience of the outer world with our ancient internal knowledge, gathered from countless lives. There is no barrier to the future and the past in the dream state; therefore the total amount and variety of information conveyed in dreams is awesome. Some of this information includes direct contact with our highest Self, precognition, past-life or future-life experiences, mythological dramas, communication with celestial beings, analysis and exploration of waking state reality, deep-rooted stresses, fears, wild humor and fantasy. All of this is wrapped up in metaphorical and symbolic experience that may or may not ever make sense to the waking state mind.

Since we are freed from the inhibitions and restrictions of our adopted world-views in dreams, they can be an excellent path for Self-knowledge. There are no accepted societal standards, no familial dictates, no ingrained defenses from our belief systems; full knowledge of spiritual Truth is therefore less hidden from us while dreaming.

The most serious consequences of our waking state Universe are the stresses that lodge in our subtle bodies; these are released during Ascension and during dreaming. To Ascend while dreaming is a powerful way to accelerate this process. Dreaming any desired dream, directing dreams in any desired direction is the natural result of expansion of consciousness. This naturally occurs when one is awake during sleep in the higher stages of enlightenment; before then, this ability develops to whatever extent awareness can be maintained while falling asleep.

Waking up while asleep (realizing that you are asleep

and dreaming) is one sign of the developing witnessing quality of Perpetual Consciousness. This form of dreaming, lucid dreaming, most often occurs during REM sleep, which comes late at night after a full night's rest. Focussing on the base of the throat while falling asleep can cause lucid dreaming: the awareness typically gathers at the base of the spine or in the heart during deep sleep and the solar plexus or throat during dreaming.

GROWTH TO FREEDOM

Dream analysis, properly undertaken can, in time, lead to complete enlightenment.

But there are faster ways. If we could only learn to interact with the Ascendant with our waking minds! Then the fulfillment of our desires would be inevitable. And instantaneous.

The Ascendant is the source of everything. Nothing lies outside it; nothing is built of anything other than it; nothing can exist for the smallest fraction of a moment outside of it. It is the conscious part of consciousness; It is the part of existence that exists. It is all that ever was, all that will ever be; you with your human nervous system have by your birth been given the ultimate gift -- a machine that can not only experience the Ascendant but direct it in any way you choose.

You are actually already directing the Ascendant all the time. But if your mind is not continually focussed on one desire at a time, your mutually contradictory thoughts and desires cancel each other out. Not entirely, of course, or else you would be a catatonic schizophrenic -- you would do nothing but sit and stare off into space. Since you are reading this, it is safe to assume you are not so self-contradictory that you are sailing in entirely useless circles in the boat of your mind.

The mind in contact with the Ascendant is like a

perfectly still pool. Thoughts and desires are like stones dropped into the pool. If one stone falls, perfectly concentric ripples spread beautifully over the water and reach the far shore. If two stones are dropped, there will be crests and valleys that cross over each other, emphasizing some, cancelling others. If a whole handful of stones hit the water at once, chaos is the result -- there is no order left. The reflection in the pond is broken into a myriad of imperfect shards. The full Moon can be sailing serenely above, but the pond will show only frenetic motion.

On any sandy beach, the kind and quality of the waves very much determine the shape of the sand. The kind and quality of our thought waves very much determine the overall shape of our minds. The ripples caused by our thoughts and desires produce both immediate (surface) and long-term (underlying) effects. When the pattern of thinking and desiring is chaotic, the result will necessarily be abnormal experiences -- mental, emotional or physical -- and abnormal behavior. The extent of the chaotic thinking directly determines the extent of the disorder in life. When the pattern of thinking and desiring is orderly, the result is health, happiness, joy, progress, creativity, fulfillment.

This may be easy to grasp intellectually regarding the individual life: if my thinking is disordered, my actions and life will be disordered. But since the Ascendant is the Source of *everything*, it is also true that my chaotic thinking will react with all parts of the Universe at all times and all places. Like salmon returning to their hatching grounds to spawn, there are no accidents of fate, there are only our own thoughts returning to their source in our individual minds.

There is quite literally no one to blame, no one to condemn, no one to judge in any way whatsoever. My desires have created my Universe, just for me; your desires have created your Universe, just for you; the fact that so many of our Universes seem so similar and seem to share many common features is a happy or a useful coincidence that defines our common humanity. (Those whose individual Universes are much out of synchrony with the majority of humanity tend to end up in mental hospitals. Or prisons.) This implies that the best cure for all disease, mental or physical, is the same -- reconnecting the individual mind consciously to the Ascendant.

The human mind is so infinitely flexible that it can stretch in its experience from the most concrete to the most abstract -- from the physical reality experienced by our senses to the abstract, internal reality of Consciousness itself.

The unifying thread of life is Love. From the most abstract to the most concrete, at every level of existence, at every level of experiencing, runs this slender thread. It seems delicate, a fragile thing, easily lost or broken, but is not so. It is more obdurate than granite; it can never be broken, never diminished, never lost; and it is forever growing, primarily by being given away. We cannot fall out of it, although sometimes we mistakenly believe that we do. Rather, what happens when we feel that we have fallen out of love is that our mutually contradictory projected desires have made it impossible for our relationship to provide further growth. This is the kindest and most accurate description. For underlying all our desires -- the melange of contradictory impulses we drop into the still waters of the Ascendant -- there forever remains our original intention, crystalline, flawless, pure, directing our being through situation after situation, life after life, world after world. And what is that original intention? It is to return to our Source. We are not and never will be at home here; we will always feel that we are the dispossessed wanderers of time. That, truly, we are. Like Pellinore of the Arthurian legends, we have lost our kingdoms and queendoms and wander aimlessly about, slowly rusting since our home has become invisible to us.

Yet is our exile self-imposed. We chose to be here; we

can choose to return whence we came whenever we so desire. Nothing can stand between us and our re-union with our Source, for we never truly left the Ascendant. We only thought we did; we have travelled exceedingly far in our imaginations, but it is fantasy merely. The Ascendant will wait patiently for us to remember throughout all Eternity if need be. For we *are* the Ascendant. No matter how long we forget this simple fact, no matter how long we adamantly deny that this is true or continue to build up false dreams and strange beliefs, the Ascendant waits patiently for us. There is no thought we can think, no action we can perform, that will ever change this simple fact. The Ascendant is the root of all that we are, it is the fullest expression of all we shall ever be; it is the Source not only of us but of everything everywhere at all times. Life, therefore, is extremely easy to understand.

If this seems difficult to grasp, it can only be because there is some part of it that has not been properly understood. It can only be because there are still some dark areas of our personalities that have not yet been addressed. How can we change this? In any way that works!

XI. THREE STAGES OF LIBERATION

Whatever you can do or dream you can , begin it.
Boldness has genius, power and magic in it.

--Goethe

PERPETUAL CONSCIOUSNESS

It is not sufficient to taste the Ascendant only during silent meditation with the eyes closed. The full development of consciousness requires a movement of the Ascendant into daily life. To accomplish this, life itself becomes the Teacher. Every desire, every conflict, every problem is an opportunity presented by this flawless and wonderful Teacher to release us from the false confines of the ego and learn that the Ascendant is the underlying Reality of everything. Once we start actively pursuing growth, every experience shows us exactly which desires and aversions maintain our past destructive behavior patterns. Every life-situation becomes an opportunity to grow toward enlightenment. As we become adept at renouncing all the previous mental constructs, we naturally develop a state of evenness that carries us smoothly over and through the mirage of Earth-life.

Permanent renunciation of the ego's constructs radically alters our experience of the world. We are no longer enslaved by past destructive behavior patterns. Since the mind is freed from dominance by thoughts about the past and the future, we naturally experience and act spontaneously in the present for the good of all creatures. Life becomes extraordinary in its simplicity -- the response to everything that comes to us is the same: acceptance, compassion and unconditional love.

The most common name in our Christian tradition for this state is "praying without ceasing." One never loses the

Infinite inner peace of perfect realization, one is always connected with the Source inside. Dr. Bucke in 1897 named this first stage of enlightenment, "Cosmic Consciousness." Since this name has been rather poorly treated in the subsequent century, we prefer to call it today, "Perpetual Consciousness." Perpetual Consciousness means that awareness of the Ascendant is permanent or perpetual.

One ancient name for this first plateau of enlightenment is *Nirvana.* Nirvana comes from the Sanskrit *Nirva,* to blow out. The fire of the ego's ignorance has been blown out because the fuel of its beliefs has been exhausted. Like a candle that has been snuffed out, all the old internal programs have been extinguished. Desire ceases to bind when every action is performed with complete consciousness, when each moment of life is lived spontaneously in the present moment. This is the natural by-product of life fully established in the awareness of the Ascendant.

Another name for Perpetual Consciousness is *Nirvikalpa Samadhi.* Nirvikalpa means "permanent"; Samadhi means, "the ultimate," or "flawless evenness." Life becomes perfectly smooth and effortless when the individuality stops attempting to control or manipulate every aspect of existence. This is the natural result of having awareness permanently established in the Infinite.

One essential characteristic of Perpetual Consciousness is known as *prajna (pragya)* in Sanskrit. Prajna is the power of the intellect that creates *witnessing.*

The nervous system is sufficiently flexible to experience the continual silence of the Ascendant and at the same time the relative states of consciousness: waking, dreaming and sleeping. This duality of awareness or witnessing is the first stage of enlightenment. Hence is pragya called the mother of wisdom.

The mind can be compared to a flock of birds that constantly changes its shape and direction and yet maintains its formation. When we begin to culture witnessing consciousness, sometimes we watch the birds fly; sometimes we are the birds. When we are both at the same time continually, we have developed prajna fully.

In the waking state, the common experience is: "I think," "I feel," "I act." This is a confusion of levels of reality. Once our awareness is permanently established in the Source, in the Ascendant, we recognize that all actions, thoughts and feelings are external to the Self. Life continues much as before, but now the individual does not mistake the source of thoughts, feelings or actions as being the individual Self. This experience of witnessing can be quite confusing to an aspirant, particularly if there is no one with sufficient knowledge available to explain what is happening. In extreme cases, it has been confused with insanity.

THE THREE GUNAS

When one experiences that thoughts, feelings, perceptions and actions continue without being caused by the Self, the question naturally arises, "Who is doing this thinking, feeling and acting?" The answer is that the fundamental forces of nature, called in Sanskrit the *gunas,* are responsible for everything in creation. I said earlier that the Ascendant is the Source of everything that is. This is true, but the Ascendant never leaves its Infinite, Ascended status to create the Universe. Where then did the Universe come from? The answer is that it came from the three gunas -- the three fundamental forces that cause everything to exist.

SATTVA

The first guna is the force of purity, the force of creative intelligence or evolution. Everything in the Universe grows, matures, becomes more complex. Sattva is the infinitely creative force which causes this to happen. In Taoism, this is called yang. Yang is positive, male, expansive, heavenly, directed outward. The primal force of sattva manifests in the individual life as clarity of thought and purity of intention. When sattva guna takes charge of an individual's life, happiness and health automatically develop. The White Ishayas model themselves as representatives of this guna of Sattva or Absolute Purity as their path on Earth.

Sattva guna manifests throughout every aspect of creation. In terms of the three relative states of consciousness, sattva is maximal in the dreaming. In terms of the three enlightened states of consciousness, sattva is maximal in Exalted Consciousness, the second stage of enlightenment. Sattva is predominant in certain foods, in certain drinks, in certain perceptions, in certain activities, in certain emotions and in certain thoughts. By gently redirecting our eating, drinking, perceiving, acting, thinking and feeling, we can turn our lives more and more in the direction of sattva. Sattva naturally increases in life as one Ascends, bringing about deep inner peace, silence, clarity, creativity, joy and perfect health. Sattva is ruled by the primal power of the Ascendant that maintains the evolutionary direction of the Universe, called in Sanskrit Narayana. In The Christian tradition, the sattvic power is represented by the Holy Spirit.

TAMAS

The opposite of sattva in every way is the guna known as tamas, or inertia. Tamas is the yin to sattva's yang -- it is negative, feminine, contractive, earthly, directed inward. Yin is the ultimate receptivity, the perfect complement to the Infinite creativity of yang. If sattva is light and white, tamas is dark and black. Tamas is represented among the Ishayas by the mysterious Black Ishaya masters who rarely appear at the monastery but dwell in seclusion and check in from time to time to keep the direction of John's Ascension flowing with his original intent.

Tamas is responsible for wisdom, intuition and the inward direction of consciousness so necessary for growth of consciousness. This is why the aspect of the Ascendant which rules tamas, Isha, is called in Sanskrit *yogiraj* -- "the King of the Yogis" -- tamas is necessary to destroy ignorance. This primal power must be in our favor if we wish to rise to complete consciousness. In the Christian tradition, tamas is represented by the Christ aspect of the trinity. Christ destroys the ignorance of the world and replaces it with the truth of pure, unconditional love, pure bliss.

Just as increasing sattva brings happiness and creativity, an imbalance of increasing tamas on Earth brings unhappiness, depression, disease and sloth. As with sattva, there are certain foods, drinks, perceptions, actions, thoughts and feelings that increase tamas. When these increase in life, life becomes sick, depressed, sad. Excessive sleep brings about an imbalance of tamas, for of the three relative states of consciousness, tamas is maximal in sleep. In the three Absolute states of consciousness, tamas is maximal in the highest degree of enlightenment, in Unity: in this state, all perception of duality has been destroyed.

RAJAS

Sattva and tamas always work together: nothing can change or evolve or even be created until the previous state is destroyed. A bud dies so a flower can bloom; a boy dies so a man can be born. The connecting link between sattva and tamas is the guna known as rajas. The Infinite tension between pure creation and pure destruction creates the third guna, the guna of energy: rajas. Rajas is neutral in direction until it is applied to creation or destruction. It is responsible for the waking state, for waking *is* activity. It is also dominant in Perpetual Consciousness, for the external world continues more or less exactly as it was in this first stage of enlightenment. Only the inner reality has opened to perception of the Ascendant: the outside continues on.

Among the Ishayas, rajas is represented by the Red Ishayas, who will be most responsible for Teaching Ascension in the world. The active Red Ishayas, guided by the purity of the Whites and aligned by the wisdom of the Blacks, will heal the world. In Sanskrit, the primal force of rajas is represented by Prajapati, the Creator. In the Christian tradition, God the Father embodies the qualities of rajas.

As with sattva and tamas, there are certain foods, drinks, perceptions, actions, thoughts and feelings that increase rajas in the life. An imbalance of rajas leads to passion, to anger, to violence. Rajas tempered by sattva bequeaths the energy necessary to achieve anything in life -- including, of course, the energy to rise to enlightenment. This is why it is said that action is the means to develop Perpetual Consciousness, but silence is the means to develop the more refined states of enlightenment.

The human world is the world of rajas: we as humans stand on the threshold of sattva *and* of tamas, capable of moving in either direction. By our thoughts and actions, we create heaven or hell of our lives. We stand on the borderline of the visible and the invisible -- living in material, physical bodies, we are nevertheless made of spirit. By our choice, we enliven the heavenly qualities of sattva or the earthly qualities of tamas. By our choice, our lives rise to joy and health or fall to unhappiness and death.

"BE WITHOUT THE THREE GUNAS."

The formula for success in life is to free oneself from the influence of the three gunas. How is this done? By Ascending -- by taking the awareness to its Source in the Ascendant. When this happens, one experiences that thoughts, feelings, perceptions and actions continue: they always were caused by the action and interaction of the fundamental forces of Nature, but now there is no longer any ego involvement, there is no longer any thought that "I am thinking, feeling, perceiving, acting." The gunas playing on the gunas give rise to thoughts; the gunas playing on the gunas give rise to feelings; the gunas playing on the gunas give rise to perception; the gunas playing on the gunas give rise to action. Thus the entire field of human life, subjective and objective, is under the dominion of the gunas.

In the waking state, we mistakenly assume authorship for our thoughts, feelings, perceptions and actions. This mistake is corrected in Perpetual Consciousness: in every experience, in every thought, in every action, the enlightened realizes that "I do not act at all." Everything comes from the gunas acting on the gunas; when this is understood, not as a dry intellectual concept but as a direct, living experience, Perpetual Consciousness is stabilized.

Perpetual Consciousness is perfect freedom: since we realize it is only the activities of nature that are causing our thoughts and experiences, we can direct our life in any way we choose. No longer subject to the old destructive internal programming, we create any new structures of habit and belief we desire. The mind, no longer caught by ego-based fearful thinking, rests in perfect inner joy. No more are we chained to past experiences or future worries; life is lived continually in the present moment. Life unfolds in perfection, for we no longer believe that our rational mind controls anything. Just as in the waking state we have no control over the hemoglobin carrying oxygen to our cells and have little ability to consciously change all the myriad electrical and chemical processes in the body, just so in Perpetual Consciousness, all of our mental processes -- thoughts, feelings, perceptions, actions -- become completely automatic. Because we have ceased undermining the perfect flowing of life from the Ascendant, everything about our individual lives becomes successful and supremely fulfilling. Life is lived in perfection.

Maharishi Patanjali, one of the earliest founders of the yoga philosophy, wrote in his Yoga Sutras nearly 5,000 years ago, "Heyam duhkham anagatam." It means that the suffering that has not yet come deserves to be avoided. How does this happen? It is a natural result of permanently establishing the individual awareness in Perpetual Consciousness. When we stop usurping the authority of the three gunas, all of life flows perfectly for us; no suffering is possible in this state.

Patanjali also noted that when we establish ourselves in *Asteya*, non-stealing, then all *ratna*, priceless wealth, presents itself to us automatically. When we stop stealing the authority for our thoughts, feelings, perceptions and actions from Nature, we have perfected Asteya. All good and wonderful things comes to those who have risen to Perpetual Consciousness, not the least of which is freedom from involuntary rebirth.

Perpetual Consciousness develops extraordinarily quickly as a result of regular Ascension. It does not take nearly as long to rewrite the internal programs as it took to create them in the first place. Fortunately! If we had to relive or consciously discreate all the horrors we have created in our minds and world, who would have the courage even to begin? Fortunately, it is not necessary. Through Ascension, we gracefully, without even being aware that it is happening, erase all the old beliefs, habits and judgments that keep life bound to the waking state of consciousness.

The typical result of five to eight years of regularly

practiced Ascension is that Perpetual Consciousness dawns in any nervous system, regardless how stressed it was at the outset. This ultimately depends on four factors:

1) How regular the individual is with his or her practice. Just as with gravity, it takes a certain acceleration to escape the pull of the Earth (9.8 meters per second squared); it takes a certain rate of acceleration to escape from the old destructive behavior patterns. This is most easily accomplished by one-pointed dedication to regularity of the practice.

2) How much stress there is in the nervous system at the beginning of the practice. Some people are a whole lot more stressed than others, due to excessive and imbalanced behavior patterns throughout their lives. Age is of course also a factor in this; the general rule is: the longer the life, the more stressed the body. The arteries of an infant look like flexible plastic tubing; the arteries of a typical octogenarian are filled with deposits and plaque, are brittle and look very much like old and rigid water supply system pipes.

3) How much stress the individual is adding to his or her nervous system every day. Some lifestyles are much more stressful than others. Regardless how efficient a filtering system, if the pond is being filled by more mud and toxic waste every day than can be removed, it will continue to decrease in quality.

4) How badly the individual wants to be free from his or her self-destructive behavior patterns. The more intense the zeal for change, the faster the change will occur. This is true for anything, of course. The more one practices the piano, the faster one learns the piano.

But all things considered, the typical average is five to eight years. It is a little surprising that it takes even this long. Where is there to go, after all? The Ascendant is already inside everyone. The reason it takes some time is simply that we are so deeply conditioned by our habitual modes of thinking, seeing and acting. Old habits tend to die hard.

EXALTED CONSCIOUSNESS

How is it possible that there can be development of consciousness beyond Perpetual Consciousness? In Perpetual Consciousness, Infinite Awareness of the Ascendant has been permanently established. Where could there be room for more growth? Logically, there cannot be. This fact has led many individuals in the past to remain "stuck" in Perpetual Consciousness. *Stuck* is in quotes in that sentence because the Eternal Freedom of Perpetual Consciousness is not accurately described as a state of non-motion, particularly when compared to the ignorance of the waking state. But compared to what else is available, remaining until death in Perpetual Consciousness *is* being stuck.

The mind is fulfilled in Perpetual Consciousness, for the blocks to the individual awareness remembering that it is Infinite have been removed. The mind therefore sees no potential for further growth. But the heart is not satisfied. Before, in the waking state, there was at least a kind of unity with the loved person or object. What was lost was awareness of the Unbounded inner Self, but at least there was a level of enjoyment in this pseudo-union.

Every level of creation has its corresponding level of happiness, even the waking state. So when in Perpetual Consciousness the mind is content with this Infinite duality between the Self and everything else, the heart feels dissatisfied, for the former unity has been lost. The mind says, "Logically, there can be no more," but the heart responds, "Wait awhile and see." There is an old saying, "The heart knows no reason." It may be completely unreasonable that there could possibly be growth past the recognition that we are Infinite, but the heart is not to be so easily defeated, not even by the Absolute!

Infinity may stand between the heart's desire, but the heart will storm the Citadel of Eternity if it must to reunite with its sundered beloved. And the heart's ally in this, of course, is that the Ultimate Reality of everything *is* Love.

The heart loves. The individual, freed from all destructive internal programs, no longer attempts to live in the past or the future and no longer sabotages the natural impulse of love. In the waking state, love rises only to be eclipsed by doubt, fear, projection and misinterpretation. There is no consistency of love in that state of consciousness, for the ego-self is never consistent. Not living in the present moment, the individual is often caught by regret, worry and fear; there is little room left for perfect, unconditional love. But love for everyone and everything spontaneously blossoms for one who lives in the present without judgments from the past or fear for the future. Since love spontaneously flows, it becomes easier and easier to love everyone and everything. This state of automatically increasing love begins to change our senses of perception: we begin to experience more and more refined levels of every object.

Even in the waking state, it is the experience that when we are in love, we don't much notice the boundaries and limitations of life. We are too busy riding the waves of enjoyment. This quality of increasing appreciation naturally opens us to the ability to love more deeply -- appreciation and love feed each other more and more easily and thoroughly once the undermining tendencies of the old belief systems have stilled.

REFINED PERCEPTION

The body has built into its wondrous structure the mechanics of much subtler styles of functioning. Approximately 90% of the material of the genetic code, for example, is encoded with no known function in the waking state. This is one of the greatest mysteries of modern genetic research: why only in the DNA is Nature, typically so ruthless in Her efficiency, squandering over nine-tenths of the building blocks? One answer is that many of these blank sections of code are non-functional only in the relative states of consciousness, waking, dreaming and sleeping. In the three enlightened states, certain parts of the DNA start functioning to create protein molecules that have no purpose in the relative states. Two of the most important of these are named *soma* and *amrita* in the ancient literature.

Soma is called the "glue of the Universe": this molecule allows us to develop perception of the subtlest level of creation, that level of reality which holds everything joined to the Ascendant. When soma increases in the body, the senses of perception gradually improve their abilities. Everything begins to be experienced in its celestial value -- the most refined level of relative structure. This is true for vision: soma allows us to see all objects filled with or made of Infinite Light, of purest Beauty. This is true for hearing: soma allows us to hear the subtlest level of sound; every sound is exquisite in its perfection. This is true for our sense of smell: every scent is redolent with fragrant wonder. This is true for touch: every physical sensation surpasses the wonder of the softest silk. This is true for taste: every bite is sweeter than the sweetest sugar, a marvel of cascading delight.

A prime result of this deeply refined level of perception is to make life supremely enjoyable. A second result can also be the ability to see and communicate with the beings that live on the subtler levels of reality: the angels, celestials, devas, elementals, gods. This state is the incarnation of magnificence: every moment is lived to the maximum. Soma transforms our clay-like bodies into temples of God's light. Celestial perception is the norm in Exalted Consciousness. Every perception *is* wonder. Truth and Beauty and Love are the handmaidens of this, the second stage of enlightenment.

Amrita is the molecule that bequeaths physical immortality. There is nothing built into the genetic code that insists the human being must age and die. There is no absolute law that the damage caused by the free radicals ranging our bodies cannot be perfectly repaired forever. Rather, every cell desires to replicate perfectly. Why does this not happen? Stress. Radioisotope studies have proven that every year *98%* of the molecules in our body are replaced. Some parts are replaced much more often: for example, the stomach lining, in terms of the molecules creating the cells, is completely new *every five days*. We have a new liver every six weeks, a new skeleton every six months, a whole new body, 100% replaced, every two years. Even the nerve cells, which themselves are not replaced after birth, are renewed every year by the changing of the atoms that compose them.

The problem is that in the waking state, we keep rebuilding the body in exactly the same way: if we have a malformed knee due to some old injury, we continue to replace the atoms in the knee in the same way so that true healing never occurs. There is no reason that this has to be so; there is no reason that life has to end at seventy-five. These are simply beliefs. We don't normally recognize them as beliefs, since they are so deep in the collective unconscious, but beliefs they are. If we change our minds deeply enough, we can become familiar with the Master Programmer, the impulse of our consciousness that determines exactly where these belief systems are being maintained. One feature of Exalted Consciousness is the ability to reverse all the old belief systems, including the belief in death. Amrita is the physical molecule that enables us to regenerate our body indefinitely.

UNITY

The final step of growth of human consciousness comes when the refined value of celestial perception melts into continual awareness of the Ascendant *on the outside*. This is the highest level of enlightenment and is known as Unified Perpetual Consciousness or Unity.

Unified Perpetual Consciousness sounds impossible from the perspective of the waking state: how can the Infinite be seen, heard, touched, tasted, smelled? It makes sense only from the standpoint of one who has risen to awareness of Infinite Consciousness on the inside, in Perpetual Consciousness. Then only does this become a practical quest. There is no resolution to our hearts' longing until every individual, every object is experienced as being the same Infinite Self that we know on the inside.

How does this final stage of growth occur? Through an act of intellectual discrimination, the enlightened individual experiences the celestial light melt into Infinity; this Infinite perceived on the outside is recognized as the same Infinite known on the inside. Said another way, the individual discovers that his Cosmic Beloved is his own Self. Funnily enough, all love ends up directed back at the Self. It is not directed back at the limited self of the waking state -- that self cannot love anything or anyone consistently -- the love is directed back at the Universal Cosmic Self of the Enlightened Mind. This results in the full awareness that each and every one is a spark of the Divine Flame, that each and every one is the same beneath all the surface differences.

What sparks this ultimate realization? Certain treatises on the subject of Unity were written by individuals in Unity: the *Brahma Sutras* of Badarayana, the *Upanishads*, the *Maharamayana* (Yoga Vasishtha) of Valmiki, *A Course in Miracles*. The entire Vedanta (literally, End of the Veda) philosophy of ancient India was designed for those in the second stage of enlightenment, Exalted Consciousness, to rise to Unity. Each of these texts is not only virtually useless in the waking state, they are potentially extremely confusing.

Another catalyst of this transformation can be the direct words of the fully enlightened to the aspirant standing at the last doorway to Unity: "Thou art That," "All this is That," "There is nothing other than That." *That* of course refers to the

Ascendant. At the appropriate instant of time, these great words (*Mahavakyas*) irrevocably crush the last taint of limitation in the mind of the evolving soul. Or this transformation can occur in a countless number of other ways; Nature Herself creates the necessary conditions so that it *must* happen.

How does individual life continue to function in Unity?

Karma (action) is divided into two types: that which is returning, regardless of our present actions, and that which lies as if dormant -- dormant because it has no chance to reach us in this lifetime. The results of our past actions are comparable to seeds. A tiny fraction of these seeds has already sprouted and is going to have effects in this life. It is as if a small amount of the storehouse of our karma has gone into building a bridge to our current existence. Beyond this bridge lies the vast majority of our past karma, comparable to mountain ranges of grain, awaiting the appropriate conditions to grow. Ascending is a divine fire which roasts these seeds so they no longer have the potential to sprout. The bridge burned, there is no longer a connection with the past; the karma no longer has the potential to return. The seeds have been roasted in the fires of wisdom.

The karma that has already sprouted creates *leshavidya,* the "last remains of ignorance." This is what keeps the body and mind functioning in Unity. The life continues on by force of habit; the individual essence is experienced as a thin, almost invisible membrane between two fullnesses: the inner Self is Infinite, the outer world is Infinite; what is left of the individuality is the faint, translucent boundary between these two fullnesses. This is what is meant in the Upanishads by, *purnam ida, purnam idam:* "This is full, that is full." This Infinite, unchanging internal experience of Eternity is not different from the Infinite, unchanging external experience of Eternity. These two fullnesses are experienced as one. This is what my Teacher meant when he said, "200% of life is the birthright of every human being."

All glories, earthly and divine, await those who are
intelligent enough to seek enlightenment.

XII. FINAL PIECES OF THE PUZZLE

As the least drop of wine tinges the whole goblet,
so the least particle of truth colors our whole life.
-- The Upanishads

Can it be difficult to expand the individual life into a permanently lived state of perfection? There can be no problem, physical, mental, emotional or spiritual, that cannot be solved by discovering our Inner Divine Nature. This is not a matter of belief, it is a necessary consequence of what our Inner Divine Nature is. No problems can withstand knowledge of the inner Self simply because no problem can co-exist with it. Where does the darkness go when we turn on the light?

FAME

What is fame? It is a magician's trick, a particularly cunning fantasy that more often than not binds the famous person into a deeper level of ignorance. Fame means that some people think someone is more important or better than everyone else. How deeply we long to be viewed as important! Is this not a hungering for love? And how vitally important each of us is! But not for the reasons we typically assume. Each one of us is vitally important because we are all a unique piece of Universal Mind -- it could be said that the Ascendant would be incomplete without any of us. But this is of course impossible, for the Ascendant can never be incomplete. Therefore each one of us is precious and necessary for the Universe to unfold as it must.

Such a cheater fame is. We are famous, we think, because of *something*. Because we make touchdowns or sing well or star in the movies. We are not famous in the eyes of the world because of our intrinsic inner worth, but because we do something well as compared with everyone else. When we no longer do that thing well, our fame vanishes like the mirage it is, leaving us with the memory of glory but nothing else. Enter here the various addictions of the world to dull the senses and help us to forget our lost moment in the Sun.

Some despair of ever becoming famous and move straight into destructive habits. Or their desire to be unique and their desire to be recognized may cause them to attempt to be famous in the field of addictions.

The entire underlying belief system that cultures the desire to be unique, special, recognized or famous is twisted, not genuine. Many of us deeply crave to prove that we are the center of the Universe, that we are loved. But unfortunately, the proof that this is so can *never* come from the outside. Those who praise you today may well damn you tomorrow; if your happiness or sense of self worth is based on others' opinions of you, your happiness will never last long. Nor will it ever be truly satisfying.

Everyone of us already possesses the most miraculous attribute that can even be conceived -- everyone is a piece of the Infinite Source. There can be no greater claim to fame than this; no action in the world can be more laudable than this; no word or thought can be more significant or meaningful than this one fact. Since built into every one of us is the greatest of all possible Realities, how can anything external matter much? Human fame comes and goes with the seasons. It is never universal. No one is ever adored by all. Caesar was despised by many. Lincoln did not win even half of his countrymen's votes in his first presidential election; he was so intensely disliked by many that his election catalyzed the most destructive war in the history of this continent. Napoleon and Hitler, on the other hand, were adored by a majority of their people.

Human fame, based on the principles of separation and specialty, is a part of the human dream that is particularly vicious. If I am better than you, you are less than I. And therefore is my Universe diminished, for my Ascendant is more in some place and less in some place else.

The truth is that all are equally unique, equally special; all deserve the greatest praise and appreciation from all. The secret here is to learn to appreciate all others. Then you are honoring the part of them that is Ideal, the part of them that is identical to the best part of you. Don't let the surface appearance deceive you: the senses are the prime agents of the dream, they are deeply committed to its continuing indefinitely. Since they are acting in consonance with their nature, they cannot be blamed for this. The senses are devised to detect variation, contrast, difference; it is not surprising some colors, shapes, words and sounds seem more pleasing and beautiful than others. But this is not Reality.

THE INNER DIVINE VOICE

There is a universal whisper pervading all of this creation. It is subtle, quiet, but it can be heard anywhere by anyone, even by the deaf. It has been called the Word, the Voice for God, the Comforter, the Holy Spirit, the Omega, the Omkara, the Primal Sound. Today many speak of the Guides or the Inner Divine Voice. The name doesn't matter. This Voice always speaks to everyone; for every question we ask, there is always an answer. Actually, there are always two answers; there is the first answer, which is created by the limited individuality. This is the answer from the ego's perspective and is usually a justification for an action or thought that we intend but question. The second answer comes from Universal Consciousness. This second is frequently called intuition; it is also sometimes interpreted as conscience. The first voice is sometimes called the voice of Satan -- the reason being that the two voices are often diametrically opposed in their advice. Whatever they are called, one voice typically speaks for the short-sighted and immediate gain of sensual gratification and experience and the second always speaks for Universal Love.

Anyone can hear the Inner Divine Voice. At times in everyone it speaks quite loudly. But if we continually ignore it or attempt to deny it, its quiet voice will seem to grow more faint, until it may seem that there is no second voice at all. What is happening in this case is that our vibratory rate is becoming more coarse, more crude; the second voice is broadcasting on a subtle channel; we are shrouding our ability to hear that channel. The human nervous system has difficulty in being tuned to more than one station at a time; if our continual habit is to listen to the voice for limitation, the second voice will fade away.

It can never vanish altogether. Since each of us is a part of the Eternal Ascendant, it is impossible ever to be apart from it in reality. But if we continually turn away from the subtle levels of experience, they will become as if silent and invisible to us.

Why is the second voice second? Because we as human beings have free will and the right to choose for ourselves what we wish to believe. The second voice is second because there was no need for *any* inner voice until the day we learned to believe that we were not part of the Ascendant, until the day we forgot that the Ultimate Reality pervades everything, our own selves included.

There is a classic series of novels by C.S. Lewis, sometimes thought of as children's stories, called *The Chronicles of Narnia*. Throughout these books, the Universal Spirit takes on the form of a magnificent lion, Aslan. Those who have not lost their ability to hear the Inner Divine Voice hear Aslan clearly speaking in a deep, richly melodious voice. Those, however, who are in the habit of choosing not to hear their Inner Counsellor hear Aslan's voice only as the roar of a huge lion. This tale is not a metaphor; it is quite literally true.

The moral extends the other way as well. If we practice

listening to the still, quiet voice within, if it becomes our habit to choose for the second voice, it becomes clearer and clearer until we can always make out its words. It may at first sound like a distant echo, a dimly remembered but inexpressibly lovely ancient song, a whisper of falling leaves, the half-heard sound of an impossibly far-off ocean; but with practice it may begin to sound like the most beautiful male or female voice ever heard. And in time it translates into an inner knowing, a certainty so powerful that the first voice fades too, not because we have drowned it out by conflicting or louder advice, but simply because it is no longer needed or desired. For those with fully purified ears, Aslan never sounds like a lion. We stand united with the Ascendant in the Indescribable Beauty of the Divine Presence. No conflicting voice (no voice at all) is needed here. Nor is thought, nor even perception. All individuality has melted back into Knowingness, into pure Being.

This is not a loss of free will or of freedom -- this is true, unending Freedom. All choice is now realized, here and now -- for the first time. Instead of acting from old self-defeating behavior patterns and belief, we stand united with the Source of all creativity and genius, free to move the Universe in any chosen direction.

IMMORTAL LIFE

Most people believe on a deep and subtle level in their own death. They have abundant proof that this will happen to them, for has it not happened to everyone else before throughout history? I had a friend once who often spoke of her death. Sometimes longing filled her voice, sometimes fear. Sometimes she wondered what it would be like to die and what should be done with her body after it stopped. I think this is a typical attitude toward the subject and is perhaps the most common.

Other people ignore their mortality and act as if they

believe they will live forever. They don't really believe that they will live forever, but they hope that if they don't think about death, maybe it will just go away and spare them. Like the proverbial ostrich, they feel that by burying all thoughts of danger, the danger will leave them alone. But the trouble with trying to cover up any thought or feeling or belief is that repression only feeds negative mental states, making them stronger.

A few believe in the possibility of physical immortality. Some of these are scientists, who analyze the basic constituents of life and see no reason the DNA cannot replicate itself perfectly forever. Others are writers and/or readers of science fiction and fantasy. And a few are saints, yogis and other spiritual visionaries who believe that it is possible to gradually transmute these gross physical bodies into material made of deathless light.

If such a phenomenon were possible, who would be likely to succeed in it? Obviously the first prerequisite for anyone is to believe it is possible. Since our thoughts create our futures, it is highly unlikely we shall experience a gradual transformation of the nature of our cells unless we at least entertain the possibility. The deeply pervading nature of the collective belief system is too extensive to be countered by mere accident.

If physical immortality is to be a realizable goal by anyone in this generation, what will be required is first of all to begin loosening the hard habits of stress, judgment and disbelief. What will be required next is to become infinitely flexible in our response to life. If there are no hard knots inside anywhere, there is no fertile field for the growth of life-threatening disease. Just as there is no room for guilt or anger if we are fully open to peace, just so, there is no room for death if we are saturated with Life. It is a waste of time and potential to die; it is the result of hardening ourselves to the natural flow of evolutionary change. People who have become old have become rigid in their bodies and their beliefs. People who stay flexible in their bodies and beliefs stay younger much longer, regardless of their chronological age.

Diet is a factor in physical health, but much more minor than many have thought. This is also true for exercise and any other of our outer actions and behavior patterns. The root of immortality is internal.

Deathlessness is neither fanciful nor difficult to achieve. In fact, it is much, much easier to continue to live than it is to die. Life is the natural state of the human, not just as a disembodied being of light, but also as an incarnate actor on the physical plane. There are certain lessons we are meant to learn here; there is no doubt that we must eventually learn them. Having learned them, there is no doubt that our purpose is to share them. Among the Ishayas, I have met several immortals.

As long as an individual keeps progressing, there is no need to go somewhere else to start over. Only when life stagnates does the necessity for disease, disaster or death manifest. If life is continually evolving in every moment, there is no need to die. This is achieved by being completely in the present moment, by being permanently established in full human awareness.

How is it possible to achieve full human awareness? We, all of us, already have awareness -- every human being already has it. The only requirement is to stop blocking it from its full free-flowing functioning. The Sun is already shining, but if there are many clouds in the way, we may fail to realize how brilliant and warm it is. The clouds will pass. The clouds always pass. This is Earth, not Venus. It is not our destiny to live shrouded forever with problems. It *is* our destiny to dance with joy in the golden light of the fully risen Sun.

Nothing depends on belief. The Sun exists; if we believe in it or not is simply not relevant. And yet, everything depends on belief. It is our beliefs which keep us enslaved. If we do not believe we can change for the better, what motivation will there be for us to do so?

DEATH

Like so much of life, this issue is one of perspective. We are all immortal souls already; this is an absolute truth, far beyond the power of any belief to increase or lessen. But through our disbelief, we are quite capable of hiding this fact from our conscious awareness. If our belief in our inevitable demise is deep enough, and if we believe that death is not just a physical transformation but certain oblivion, it is quite possible to spend a long time after our body's death experiencing only one thing -- the rather depressing awareness that we are dead.

Our afterlife may be curiously twisted in other ways by our deep-rooted beliefs. We may create an entire world, peopled with a myriad of beings, with which we interact exactly as we do here -- the one exception being that as our attention strays, our mind-created world dissolves around us. Every day we go to work and lay a brick wall, never noticing the bricks disappear back into mind-stuff as we move down the line. Created in the image and likeness of the Ascendant, we all have infinitely powerful minds, capable of doing anything.

Or we can be so attached to our human body or to another person or even to a house or a garden that we refuse to abandon it. This is the usual source of ghosts -- those disincarnate spirits who have not yet remembered their freedom and are still attached to their pasts.

But the most common after death experience is a quick return to a world ideally suited to the condition of our beliefs at death. It will be a world more heavenly than this one if our thoughts here have been more heavenly than the thoughts that brought us here. Similarly, it will be a world worse than this if our thoughts have been darker than those that created our present body. It is not necessary to look to other planets to find a vast variety of heavenly and hellish fates -- they are already present here on our Earth. The amazing number of different futures available on Earth -- well over five billion human souls at this writing -- shows the huge number of possible existences on just this one small planet. And there are more than 200 billion suns in this galaxy alone! And at least one thousand billions galaxies in this Universe, many much larger than ours! And who can even begin to guess how many Universes may exist in the Infinite regions of Divine Mind?

I have heard that Carl Sagan demonstrates the size of our known Universe thus: picking up a handful of sand from a beach, he says that the number of grains of sand in his hand are roughly equivalent to the number of stars in our galaxy. The number of grains of sand in every beach on the Earth is the rough equivalent of the number of stars in the known Universe. It is vast beyond any human ability to conceive. Small wonder, then, that the number of potential afterlife states is indeed enormous.

Small wonder too that a tiny percentage of possibility is not zero. It may be that few indeed have mastered the Earth-life sufficiently to negate the necessity of death. But even a small percentage is not the same as zero, is it?

THE FINAL JUDGMENT

As many people are alive today as have ever lived throughout recorded history. One reading of the Bible says that everyone who has ever lived throughout recorded history is alive today. If this is true, why would it be so? Logically so that the so-called "Final Judgment" can occur. What is this Final Judgment? In terms of this Earth, it may partly mean that those who wish to remain in immortal bodies may do so now. It may also partly mean that those who wish and believe that they must die to continue on having the opportunity to do so. This planet is moving into a phase of immortality. But there are many mansions in my Father's garden; there is a place for everyone.

The concept of eternal damnation is a particularly strange belief of the human ego, that force typically called Satan in the West. Fortunately, there is not the slightest scrap of Reality in it. It is a bizarre fantasy created by sleeping human minds. The Final Judgment has nothing at all to do with such strange dreams. God is Omnipresent and Eternal. Where then the potential ever to be away from Him? There is none. Only our beliefs can color our perception to be unaware of this simple fact. Only our beliefs can cause us pain. Only our beliefs can cause our deaths.

My hope and belief is that a large number will join with the Ishayas and the other Teachers walking on the Earth today and choose to remain here for the ascent of perfection. Why choose to die and do it all over again? Why deny the nectar and the ambrosia? Why renounce the living water of the present for the pestilent well of the past? Our human lives can be filled with pain and hell or they can be filled with life and Heaven. We have free will. I pray you will all join with us; together we can re-create this world in the image and likeness of the Ascendant. Let us save this planet at this last second, at this final stroke before the tolling of the midnight bell! Let us be part of the solution rather than the problem. Let us unite with the upward current of creation and Heal together rather than destroy separately. Let us be one together. Let us grow upward into the light of Truth and Joy together.

Come with us and let us take your sorrow and your pain and give you peace, joy and health. You have the full potential of God inside you. We don't want your money, we don't want your goods or possessions, we don't want anything from you other than for you to realize who you are. You are the sons and daughters of the Ascendant. This is not a difficult truth to realize; in fact, it is infinitely easier to realize this than to continue to deny it. But you must take the first step. You must be willing to let go of your past, your beliefs in limitation and disease and death. You must be willing to be baptized in the fires of purification and knowledge and experience in order to move ahead.

This need not be a painful birth. It will be painful only to the extent that you attempt to hold onto your old beliefs and concepts. Once the willingness is there to drop *everything* that was falsely created by the ego, the ride becomes smooth. Only if you try to hold onto your possessions of material or belief can there be pain.

Don't read this in a small or limited way! It is possible to own the whole world and be enlightened. There is no guarantee that the monk who has renounced the world is more evolved than the king on his throne. In fact, he may be considerably less evolved. True renunciation occurs in the mind. If this must also occur on the physical plane is determined by how deeply the roots of attachment spread inside. If they are shallow, nothing need be given up. If they are deep, giving up everything may not help.

What does help is the practice of Ascension. In whatever form it comes into the life, a true act of Ascension cuts the bondage with the material world, with the beliefs and judgments that keep the human mind coarse and crude. A true act of Ascension liberates the spirit to the direct experience of its own essential Nature. Anything that causes this to occur is Ascension, if it is taught formally by the Teachers of Ascension trained by the Ishayas or not. Liberation from the confines of the ego is much bigger than any system of inner development, regardless how divinely inspired and cleverly created.

XIII. REVIEW: TWO WAYS TO LIVE

Love or fear, which do you choose?

There are basically only two ways to view the world, our relationships with others, and ourselves. Every thought, feeling or perception is either based in fear or in love. Everyone we meet, every situation we experience, every feeling we have is rooted in either love or fear. This extends from individual reactions inside each of us to global realities -- war, politics, economics, belief systems of all kinds.

For example, nations that base their thinking in fear will attack or be attacked by others. Most, if not all, of the countries in the world today are operating primarily from fear. Each year, enormous wealth is devoted to the tools of war -- the resultant loss to other areas of human endeavor is inconceivable. Japan and Germany, forced since their defeat in WWII to be essentially non-violent, have experienced unparalleled economic growth and today largely dominate the world marketplace. Switzerland, usually at peace with herself and the world since the first clans came together at Lake Lucerne in 1291, boasts more millionaires per citizen than any other country. How much richer would we all be if we had not been such a violent race?

But what of aggressive nations? Is it not our duty to protect the innocent? Did not the Nazis and then the communists need to be confronted, contained, defeated?

This argument is like examining a single piece of a complex object to discover what it is. Imagine six blind men asked to stretch out their hands to feel one small area of an elephant and then told to describe what an elephant is. One touches only the tusk and declares that elephant is another name for a spear. Another touches the tail and *knows* that elephants are ropes. The man touching the leg is certain elephants are trees and so on. Each is perfectly correct in their interpretation of the specific information supplied, but woefully wrong in terms of the whole.

Similarly in terms of world events. If you have already cut off an arm, of course you must apply a tourniquet to keep the patient from bleeding to death. The point is that there was never the necessity of cutting off an arm.

Hitler and the other political aggressors of history have never acted without help and support from others. If they had attempted to act alone, the mental hospitals would have locked them up long before they could have caused anyone else any trouble. The vibratory rate of the Germanic speaking peoples produced Hitler. The collective desire or race consciousness of the people of the world created the necessary preconditions for the Second World War, just as has been the case for every war since human beings started having wars.

Let me share a story of the Ishayas with you.

Long ago, there was a beautiful nation, a city-state of unprecedented wisdom and peace. Perhaps, if you look deep enough into the collective memory of humanity you carry around in your DNA, you can touch the sweet memory of this wonderful place. Our most pleasant myths from the past -- Atlantis, Lemura, Bharata, Xanadu, Camelot -- are but the shadowy remnant of this magical home. It was more than beautiful; perfect happiness and peace were the norm; the joy of the people was in following the highest good for themselves and for everyone else. It was a land of prosperity and progress unequalled by anything in our histories or even our fantasies, and the simple truth is that it lasted for a very, very long time.

But like the echo of distant thunder, a cloud rose on the horizon of our fabulous paradise. Another people, beyond the furthest borders, envied the wealth and beauty of our civilization and decided to conquer it.

Here we made a fundamental error. We could have educated and assisted the barbarians. The world was large enough, we were wise enough, they were as children before our glory -- but instead we chose to respond to them as if they really could have harmed us. We built walls to keep them out and erected defenses on all our borders.

In time, because we had given away our strength, our perfect harmlessness, our civilization rotted from the inside. In time, what we strove to protect was hardly anymore worth saving. In time, the barbarians grew powerful enough to breach our defenses and destroy us. Perhaps you remember now how this happened: we created this fall; we created our degenerative disease; we created our death.

This is today a constantly recurring reality. How often do we feel victimized, abused, taken advantage of? How often do we feel our anger is justified? How often must we seek revenge for the dreadful wrongs committed against us? How often must we protect ourselves so that we will not be further harmed?

There is another way of living. The first step is to realize that we, each of us, create our own world. We each, by our moment-by-moment decisions, determine our present reality and our future fate. This may not appear immediately obvious. How did I create my own Universe if I am born addicted to cocaine, for example? Where is the love in such a nightmarish, addicted birth?

Again, this is a case of looking at a small piece of the energy stream that is an individual's relationship with the Ascendant. From the standpoint of Universal Mind, there is no punishment, no crime to be punished, no sinner to be saved. There are only lessons to be mastered. Every person on the Earth today is an individual expression of Universal Mind. Each is like the finger on a hand. How can a finger be bad or wrong? If it slips and the hand is cut, will the other fingers punish it? This idea is of course absurd. But when we think of individual humans, we have somehow come to the strange conclusion that some of us as individuals have the right to judge, criticize and condemn some of the other individuals alive today.

But what of protecting others? If an individual is damaging himself or others, surely he needs to be stopped?

It is all a matter of perspective. Imagine for a moment that the typical perception of a human being is falsely limited. Imagine, if you will, that this limited perception is recognizing only the tiniest fraction of Reality and that this limited perception is a fundamental error. Stretch your mind with me as I softly suggest that we are multi-dimensional beings, that the three commonly perceived dimensions are not by any means the whole of the story. What then of our space-time-causation bound judgments about reality?

Perhaps an analogy will help.

Imagine the senses of a being limited to only two dimensions. How difficult it would be to know the purpose of any three-dimensional object. Even the pen in my hand would seem miraculous to a two-dimensional person living on my writing tablet. The point of the pen disappears from the familiar boundaries of the two-dimensional reality, flies through an unknown dimension, re-appears in a different place, performs strange, incomprehensible actions, then disappears again.

Two-dimensional slices of the pen would yield little more information; cross-sections taken from any place would be virtually meaningless. Even if a map could be made of all the cross-sections of the pen, it would still be all but impossible to understand what it was. The two-dimensional beings might think it was God, for the pen performs miracles continually. Or they might think it was Satan, particularly if the ink from the pen was misplaced from their perspective. But they would never understand the pen as we do.

The point is that if we as human beings are not in fact limited to the three-dimensional reality that our senses reveal to us, then the rational laws we have applied to judge guilt and innocence *must* be false -- from a higher dimensional perspective. The frightful concerns of the child are seen by the mature adult as being easy to solve. A young boy cries in agony and fear when the wheel falls off his favorite truck. The father, seeing that it is only a toy, sympathizes deeply, perhaps chuckling slightly that something so small and inconsequential could cause such a fuss -- but what will the same father do if the wheel falls off *his* truck?

The criminal, judged by his peers as worthy of imprisonment or death, from a higher-dimensional perspective is an energy stream of immortal life acting out all possibilities in his/her required sequence of growth back home. Roots of a tree go in many directions and deep to create the basis for a powerful and dynamic living structure.

A given entity may choose a life that is viewed as bad or sinful by the majority of humanity simply to learn humility or compassion, or to curb self-importance, or occasionally to help others caught by the belief systems of our cultures.

I am certainly not condoning crime. There is no lasting value in behavior that is damaging to one's self or others. I am only saying that when we find ourselves condemning or judging others -- and this is true if the judgment is large or small in our eyes -- then we are looking from a limited perspective, without understanding the whole picture. This is always true. Either the Universe is perfect, filled throughout every particle with love and the Omniscient wisdom of the Ascendant Mind, or else it is flawed, imperfect, filled with pain, sorrow, suffering, error, death.

It may sound surprising to state this fundamental dichotomy so plainly. Most tend to believe that, although there is much of good in life, there is also much of evil, much that is wrong with our individual lives and with the world as a whole. Crime, disease, war, death -- these are indisputable facts of the Earth life. There may exist other places or perhaps other times when these realities do not or did not exist, but certainly no one can argue that these intensely evil or at least painful and sorrowful facts are not a part of our world of today. Like it or not, these are the indelible markings of a dark and powerful mind working in and throughout our world. Or if these abundant proofs do not conclusively demonstrate a conscious mind of malicious intent, they certainly must at least prove that we live in a Universe where Natural Law sometimes supports and nourishes but also often destroys -- perhaps so that life as a whole will continue to progress, or perhaps simply because Natural Law unconsciously functions with no regard for the individual entities affected by its action.

I hope you are investing this inquiry with emotional intensity. If you aren't, perhaps you'd like to see if you can conjure up some resentment or anger or pain. Perhaps you would like to review for a moment all the terrible wrongs of the past and present in our world. Or take a moment to recall all the frightful wrongs and injustices you or someone close to you has experienced. Think of the early death of a loved one, of the horrible disease that caught another you cared for and caused him or her to suffer intensely. Reflect for a moment how terribly unjust God must be to permit all the pain and agony we human beings and even the plants and animals are forced to experience here on Earth. Doesn't it make you deeply sad? Doesn't it make you want to cry out in rage at such an uncaring God? Don't you sometimes sob your frustration to the uncaring void? What is wrong with the Universe, anyway? How could these things have happened! Why did God make such a horrible place!

If you are now feeling some degree of frustration for your life or the life of the world as it is here and now, we may be able to begin to make some progress in this direction. What we wish to do is identify the dark feelings so that we can be free of them. You must be able to see an enemy before you can fight him!

The following is another old story, found in several ancient cultures, that the Ishayas like to tell.

One day God decided to come to Earth to see exactly how His children were doing. He did not try to hide His presence, but went about quite openly as God in human form. Some recognized Him at once and greeted Him with love, but many who knew perfectly well who He was ignored Him, and a few even tried to kill Him.

Afterwards, when all involved had died as humans, one of those who had loved God as He walked on the Earth was surprised to find those who had hated God in His human form and tried to kill Him were also in Heaven with those who had loved Him.

"How can this be?" he asked, incredulous. "Is it not better to love than to hate?"

"Assuredly," God answered, smiling. "But I prefer being hated to being ignored!"

Hate is at least a movement of energy. It is far better to feel your anger, your despair, your frustration than to try to lock it away somewhere inside. The human spirit is an extremely flexible medium. If we push something down here, it will pop up over there, just like those toys that so many little children love so much. They hammer away at the colored sticks, then laugh in glee when, having forced one down here, another pops up over there. We force down some undesirable feeling or characteristic, and immediately half a dozen more erupt in our lives to fill the vacuum. We finally manage to curb our drug or alcohol problem and find we're smoking three packs of Camels a day. Or we finally end our thirty-year addiction to tobacco and find to our dismay that we have gained a hundred pounds.

Repression alters and twists our thoughts, feelings and behaviors, Honest recognition and release frees us from future suffering. The human mind does not like to be forced.

Here is another story from the Ishayas:

Once a king of a city-state was bothered by monkeys. They were so numerous and bothersome that no one could do any business; the crops were continually being eaten; the merchants' wares were constantly being stolen; the artisans' crafts were forever being molested. The king, desperate for a solution, committed the full resources of his realm to the extermination of the monkeys. But for every one killed, it seemed two more came from the jungle -- a vacuum was being created that the monkeys kept filling. It was hopeless; his realm bankrupt, the king ended his life in poverty and despair.

His eldest son had watched all of this in dismay. When he ascended the throne, he decided that, rather than trying to kill the monkeys, he would see if there was some way to have them be of assistance to the kingdom. His first act was to try to befriend them -- he planted grove upon grove of bananas and plantains. A surprising thing happened -- the monkeys were so busy enjoying the fruit that they stopped having time to bother the citizens. And when a neighboring kingdom invaded, the monkeys fought savagely to defend their land.

Trying to undermine our thoughts and feelings by repression is like trying to kill the monkeys. Allowing the mind to express its feelings and thoughts is like feeding the monkeys. Is it not obvious which technique is preferable?

If we harbor feelings of frustration or anger within, it will be quite natural and inevitable to see the world as if it were a frightening place. We will feel as though we are victims and act accordingly. Convinced that the world is a hostile, harsh environment, we may conclude that the only way to be safe is to attack first, thus to protect ourselves from being attacked. Or we may become sullen and habitually angry, or we may internalize our frustration, anger and despair to such an extent that we damage our health. High blood pressure does not come from eating too much salt or smoking too much but from a state of mind. Heart disease, cancer and a host of other diseases follow in the wake of our belief in an evil or at least thoughtlessly cruel world.

It is necessary to recognize the enemy. The enemy is not

"out there" somewhere; the enemy is not an external agent, not a bacteria, not a carcinogenic substance, not a degenerative disease; the enemy is not time; the enemy is not scarcity of resources; the enemy is not anything outside. The enemy is with us always: the enemy is our own beliefs and judgments about the nature of the world and our personal lives.

This one fact, if it can be properly understood, can provide great hope to us. If our beliefs are responsible for our lives, then we can change our belief structure. If we change our beliefs, our perceptions and actions will necessarily change.

The problem is that changing our beliefs is not usually accomplished by simply deciding that they are no longer serving us. They are rather more intimate and sticky to us and harder to change than our cars or homes. If we realize that our car doesn't run well and is too expensive to fix, it is usually fairly easy to turn it in on another. And if we outgrow our house, there is not much of a shortage of homes on this planet. Our beliefs, on the other hand, are deep inside, quietly running, influencing our every thought and action long before we are aware that we are continually deciding to see and experience the world as we do. How, then, to change beliefs?

NEW EXPERIENCE

Typically beliefs change as the result of new experience. How does new experience come to us? The first step is to introduce a faint doubt into our rigid belief structure. A small spark can start a huge fire if the conditions are right. The small spark needed to burn our old belief system and transform our lives is the faintest feeling, deep inside, that maybe everything that we have thought and believed about life and the Universe is false. What if, after all, there is more to life than we have yet perceived or understood? What if -- just perhaps -- those we have been listening to for all these years really do know next to nothing? What if our potential Reality is actually so much more rich and wonderful than we have ever dreamed? What if?

With even such a quiet and faint initial opening to a more expanded level of understanding, change begins and accelerates in our lives. Books start leaping off the shelves at us. As if by magic, people unlike any we have ever known start appearing to us to befriend us and Teach us. The old world starts to drop away faster and faster as the new life develops inside.

Deeper knowledge and ever-expanding experience step forth to assist us now. There exist systematic, mechanical and all but effortless techniques to begin to raise our consciousness, to open us ever more fully and completely to Universal Mind.

We of the Ishaya Tradition teach a series of such techniques. These are not the only techniques that are effective, but they do work extremely well and quickly to bring out a complete transformation of personal experience. This process we call Ascension; it is a guided, step-by-step procedure for rising to a full appreciation of Universal Mind. The practice is not in any sense difficult; it is normally practiced for a few minutes two or three times a day.

Introductory courses are offered during weekends or weeknights by appointment. The results of these courses are immediate, obvious, profound.

Intermediate courses in Ascension are also offered; these typically range in length from a week to six months. These courses extend and stabilize the ability to experience and utilize the Ascendant. In the Pacific Northwest, a six month in-residence course to train Teachers of Ascension is available every year beginning in January. The world desperately needs the knowledge of how to rise effortlessly beyond self-defeating beliefs and judgments and experience the full potential of the individual life.

There are no requirements to practice Ascension -- it is not necessary to change any beliefs, it is not necessary to change your lifestyle, it is not necessary to change your habits. It may be that you will be one of those who quietly enjoys the benefits of deep relaxation, improving health and expansion of consciousness without engaging in any courses after the first. That is fine -- there are no pressures from our side to take further classes or even to continue Ascending regularly. The suggestion is simply for you to come, try an Introductory Course; if you wish to leave it at that, so be it. But if you wish to pursue it more deeply, that option is also available.

We unreservedly recommend this knowledge to everyone; in our experience, everyone can benefit from it. Ascension is a gradual unfolding of knowledge through experience. Each of the courses offers techniques which are more advanced than the preceding. The rate of progress accelerates through each of the courses as the individual's level of stress diminishes and the experience of consciousness expands.

Even though this is true, the first technique offered in the very first course is sufficient to enlighten anyone, regardless how stressed, depressed or pessimistic. The advanced techniques accelerate progress but are not required. The first course is sufficient to bring the light of the Ascendant fully to conscious awareness for anyone who is willing to practice the technique regularly.

The reason this is so is because the Ascendant *is* universal; it is found inside as well as outside of everyone and everything. Since this is so, two things are surprising: first, why is the Infinite light of the Ascendant not the common experience of everyone? Second, why should a technique of any kind be required to experience it?

Habit is an answer to the first question. It is our habit to use our senses in an outward direction. Whenever we open our eyes and see, whenever we touch, hear or feel, these are "vertically" outward motions of the mind. This is the first lesson the infant needs to learn in order to interact with the environment. Those who fail in developing (or retaining) this outward direction of the mind end up in mental wards. It is also our habit to think in a "horizontal" direction -- that is, we think *about* things, we contemplate the nature of reality, we daydream, we flow around the surface of the mind thinking about life. One purpose of school is to develop this horizontal angle of the mind.

Both of these directions of the mind are considered normal, common, routine, completely natural. But we often believe that the only remaining direction, "vertically" inward, is difficult or impossible and must require tremendous ability to concentrate or control the mind.

Rarely do we allow our perceptions or thoughts to move vertically inward, to seek more abstract or universal levels of understanding. And yet, how can this be difficult? The frequency of peak experiences is an indication that it is not hard to develop the mind. People everywhere throughout history have tasted higher consciousness; their experiences have come at the most peculiar times and places: over a crowded desk, staring at the stars in January, at the beach, during childbirth; the catalogue is as endless and extensive as is the human race itself.

All that is necessary to begin to move to higher levels of consciousness is to begin to retrain the mind to move vertically inward.

Why is a technique required to learn to re-groove the brain into a new, inwardly vertical habit pattern? This is like the art of speaking. Learning to manipulate our breath, vocal cords, tongue and mouth in such a way as to communicate meaningful symbols to other similar beings is something we naturally learn to do. This is something we take for granted. Yet we had to learn how to do it. It never ceases to amaze most of us how small children of other countries speak fluently a language that we as adults only with great effort can poorly mimic. It is not difficult to speak, but we have to learn how to do it. Similarly with walking or any other acquired skill. Certainly these activities are for all practical purposes natural; just as certainly, we had to learn how to do them.

The mind is a wonderfully complex machine that can be trained to do a staggering variety of things. Just so, it can be trained to move vertically inward. The techniques of Ascension accomplish this.

The mind can easily be taught to experience the Ascendant. That a technique of some kind is required to do this is not literally true. There have been numerous examples of rapture or spontaneous experience of at least a temporary movement in the direction of the Ascendant throughout world history. Even a short experience of inner light, of perfect peace, of unlimited joy, of knowingness frequently changes the experiencer permanently. Massive belief systems are often created or adopted from the most temporary of flashes of altered perception.

That this kind of experience can and does happen spontaneously proves that it is completely natural. The universality of the experience is demonstrated by the fact that practically everyone at some point in life has had at least a taste of higher consciousness. Almost all of us have had at least a glimpse beyond the veil of relative life. I might be so bold as to say that everyone has had such an experience, but some of us have chosen to forget it or misinterpret it. The reasons for this inability to recall may vary from individual to individual, but are usually based in fear.

When I was young, in my teens, I often experienced higher consciousness knocking on my door when I was studying late at night in the kitchen -- it was the warmest room in the house and perfectly quiet after everyone else was in bed. With my books spread out everywhere all over the kitchen table, quite often I had to force myself to read them or write my assignments, for I felt a huge presence just outside the room that wanted in and wanted to be recognized -- why? I did not know, but it was terrifying to me. This force was huge, awesome, powerful -- and it wanted me to be aware of it. Was it the devil? Was it a disincarnate spirit? My father, perhaps, returning from beyond the grave? Or was it a demon?

Only years later did I learn that I was afraid of my own higher Self, trying to open the locked doors in my mind. I believe this is actually a common experience; I believe also that many people have been so terrified by similar experiences they have tried to shut down their minds into extremely narrow and rigid boundaries. One tragedy of modern life is that so many have so well succeeded in their attempt. The world would be a much healthier place if these individuals (who are actually quite highly evolved) would give up their fear of their own perfection. They would then start to be part of the solution instead of the problem.

The peak experience is common in the human being, a natural fluctuation of consciousness. But to make it regular and repeatable, to make it a permanent, all-time reality that is welcomed and accepted and enjoyed, two factors are required by most people. First, it must be understood. Few of us willingly accept a stranger into our homes without knowing something about him or her. What is the experience of higher consciousness? Why does it occur? What value does it have? If the answers to these questions are mastered, there is no difficulty in flinging open the doors we have bolted shut; the experience of higher consciousness rushes in like a river after the dam containing it has broken.

The second requirement for stabilizing higher consciousness, required by most, is a practical method to systematically train the mind to experience the inner light.

What must such a technique be like? First and ideally, it will not engage our belief systems. If the experience of higher consciousness is in fact universal, it should be capable of being experienced by anyone from any religious, political or economic background. And the technique should not be so complex that only those with giant intellects can utilize it. Nor should it require such transcendental devotion that only those with wonderfully exalted hearts can pierce through their ignorance and touch the Heart of God. The universal requirement of this age is that the experience be open to all. Anyone from any walk of life should be able to practice the techniques and derive the desired result.

Another all-important reason for not involving our belief systems is that it is exactly our belief systems -- our habits and judgments about the nature of life -- that are keeping our experience of life exactly as it is. Something new is required to break out of the mold of our past. The "Aha" experience comes from unexpected, dramatic and thorough change of perspective; without warning, the old habit patterns are relaxed and a different vista is revealed. This is sudden, complete, wonderful.

The Ascension techniques fulfill these requirements. They are systematic. They are simple to understand and practice. They involve no changes of beliefs or lifestyle. They involve no beliefs! And they are wonderfully effective at removing the stresses that block the perception of inner reality. Regular practice of Ascension produces manifold changes in life, based on personal, direct experience.

The invitation is try an introductory course and see for yourself. Practice the first technique regularly for a month or so and see what happens to you. Many others have reported wonderful growth and improvement in every area of life from Ascension. What do you have to lose by trying?

XIV: THE SCIENCE OF ASCENSION

In this practice, no effort is lost.

This is an age of fear. We are afraid of other countries, other humans, and ourselves. It is rare to feel safe ever -- and no amount of physical manipulation increases our sense of security. Buying one more set of bolts and locks for our doors does not much protect us from our neighbors; building yet another and more advanced weapons system does not defend our borders so much better that we feel permanently at peace. Lacking firm conviction in our own invincibility, we turn to the external world with doubt, hoping -- against all logic and previous experience -- that we shall remain secure.

What is the essence of security? How does one become truly fearless? What are the mechanics of peace?

The Science of Ascension involves a process of systematic unlearning. From birth, we have all structured certain beliefs, based on our own direct experience. If we are burned by a hot stove, we quickly learn to believe that fire can hurt us. We structure beliefs about the range of temperatures our bodies can safely withstand; we culture other beliefs about the nature of our bodies and how they can be damaged.

Some of our beliefs are obviously useful to continuance of our physical lives. It is useful to remember how to drive our car without having to reread the owner's manual each time we sit behind the wheel. It is useful to remember which house is ours each time we wish to return home without having to ask our neighbors. It is usually useful to recognize our children when we see them.

But it is also true that other beliefs are self-defeating and counter-productive. If we believe we are failures, this is the kind of experience we will continually draw to us. If we believe that life is hard, that we are unloved and perhaps even unlovable, that we are unhappy, that we are unworthy, will we experience an easy, effortless life of love and joy? Only by changing our underlying networks of belief can we hope to experience the future we -- at least intellectually! -- would prefer.

Unmaking or unlearning old belief patterns is extraordinarily difficult by consciously attempting to unmake them or change them. Any psychoanalyst will testify to the great difficulty inherent in changing even one self-concept through the traditional approach of analyzing the root cause of any abnormal behavior pattern. It may appear a gargantuan, highly frustrating, even impossible task to rewrite our personalities by consciously choosing to do so. For most of us, it might well prove impossible.

In this country, the high percentage of mentally ill people, both committed and uncommitted, is abundant proof that our modern society is not a healthy place in which to live. And this also demonstrates that our mental health practitioners are not successful in their chosen professions. Ditto for the physical diseases that afflict the modern world. In ancient China, every physician was required by law to list on a placard outside his office the number of his patients who had died that year. The purpose of the physician was to Heal. Only those who were successful Healers were permitted to continue the practice of medicine.

In the attempt to root out the source of the problems that cause physical or mental imbalance, a great deal of effort is wasted and the results are usually marginal at best. Doctors, counsellors and patients continue following this approach simply because nothing better has been widely available.

But it is possible to change deep-seated belief patterns easily and effortlessly. This is done by the introduction of a few new seed thoughts. These seed thoughts have the unique and invaluable characteristic of systematically and effortlessly expanding the conscious boundaries of the individual's mind. Each of these seed thoughts has the result of unmaking past belief patterns that keep our lives from unfolding in a healthy and harmonious way. Each of these seed thoughts, correctly practiced, causes the entire range of the personality to become aligned with the most basic force in the Universe. Any individual, correctly practicing over a long enough period of time, effortlessly and systematically rises beyond his previous restrictive beliefs and habit patterns into a new and much more beneficial style of functioning of his/her nervous system.

The Science of Ascension is a systematic and graduated methodology for developing the mind. "Ascension" means to rise above. What happens during the practice of Ascension is that the individual rises above his/her previous state of conscious awareness and begins to experience the higher states of appreciation of Reality that lie hidden inside.

This creates a state of problem-free living. "Problem free" does *not* mean challenge-free: life does not become flat or passive; problem-free *does* mean that inner stability is greater than any challenge from life; the inner creativity available for use is greater than any problem. Any challenge can be and is met and solved in the simplest, most graceful and most beneficial way once this state has developed.

The mechanics of Ascension are quite simple. What is necessary is to learn how to listen: to the people in our Universe, to our world, to our bodies, to our minds, to our hearts. Every moment of every day we are being told everything we need to know to live in complete freedom, harmony and joy. From fear, we usually choose not to hear. Our judgments of limitation, of good and evil, have chained us into small lives of pain and suffering. To be free, it is necessary to acknowledge what we have done and are continuing to do to ourselves to keep from listening. This can be a painful process, but it does not have to be.

FOUR ASCENSION ATTITUDES

There are four basic emotions or Attitudes that lead to Ascension: Appreciation, Gratitude, Love and Direct Cognition. There are thousands, even millions of specific applications of these four basic Ascension Attitudes. For example, any feeling of love for anyone or anything tends, to some greater or lesser degree, to cause the vibratory rate of the individual to rise, to expand the conscious capacity of the mind, to improve the health of the body, to decrease the boundaries of life. If you think of any time you have been sincerely in love, you will probably remember how easy it was to overlook the small, surface flaws of your beloved and to focus on his/her perfection and beauty. This is an example of expanding awareness, but such occurrences are typically not consistent or powerful enough to transform life permanently.

Even repeated and regular attempts to Ascend through prayer, a form of the Direct Cognition Ascension Attitude, are typically not ultimately transforming to the life. The reason for this is not necessarily from any lack of commitment or dedication on the part of the praying person. There are usually three causes for this common failure. The first is the limited amount of time spent in prayer. If, for example, an hour a day is spent attempting to move to a higher vibrational frequency and the other twenty-three hours are spent either staying on the same mental plane or going backwards, how can it be surprising that the attempts fail? Even if the entire hour is one-pointedly directed to moving higher, there are still twenty-three hours with quite a different focus. If one out of every twenty-three thoughts are directed upwards and the other twenty-three are directed horizontally or downward, can it be surprising that life doesn't quickly improve?

The second cause of failure usually comes from conflicting desires. One part of the personality may sincerely desire an answer to a problem, but another part may, perhaps even secretly, be desiring the opposite. For example, a miraculous cure may be the object of prayer, but were such a cure to come, the rest of the personality might be terrified. Or it might not feel itself worthy of such a solution. ("Why should God waste a miracle on such as me?") In such a state of conflicting desires, no clear answer is the most likely response from Nature.

The third cause of failure is that the content of the prayer is often simply not effective. This can take a vast number of forms. Of the thousands of possible applications of the four primary Ascension Attitudes, only a surprisingly small number are either extremely effective or universal in application. In the Ishayas' experience, approximately one hundred and eight of these are the best for everyone; of these one hundred and eight, twenty-seven are all that we commonly teach, for these twenty-seven are the most powerful, easy to use, and lead most directly and quickly to the desired goal. These twenty-seven are taught by the Ishayas' Teachers of Ascension in a systematic and verifiable manner, with individual practice and progress interlaced with further instructions in the techniques. This way establishes tangible results as the strongest reinforcing agents for continued practice.

Each of the twenty-seven Ascension Attitudes possesses the quality of immediate feedback -- that is, the effect of practice is immediately noticeable. The reason for this is that each of the twenty-seven has the extraordinary and unique characteristic of allowing the mind automatically to continue Ascending to ever higher levels of experience and understanding.

As such, even the first of the twenty-seven Ascension Attitudes is sufficient to liberate any human being fully. The advantage of having more than one tool in the tool chest is that the mind sometimes tricks itself into activating slower loops. This happens primarily because of past desires and beliefs that life is or should be difficult and/or painful. Having more than one Ascension Attitude is like an insurance policy. If the force of ancient habit is too deeply entrenched (and for most in this modern world, it seems to be), more than one angle of Ascension will be required.

In our experience, it is extremely doubtful that any individual could resist the power of this small handful of twenty-seven Ascension Attitudes for long. This is true because each of the twenty-seven has the inherent property of leading the mind into ever-higher rates of experience and understanding; simultaneously, each of the twenty-seven assists the mind to undo *all* of its false beliefs, fears and imaginings. Each of the twenty-seven wipes the slate of the mind clean while writing there a new script. The old internal programs cannot long resist the power and clarity of the new.

The Ascension Attitudes involve no religious beliefs; indeed, they involve no beliefs of any kind. They are universal. They violate no creed or established faith. They can be equally well practiced by the Christian, the Muslim, the Hindu, the Buddhist, the Jew, the agnostic, the atheist. They tap into universal human states and inspire Ascension from wherever one happens to be.

THREE QUALITIES OF ASCENSION

Each of the Ascension Attitudes has three aspects. First, there is an emotional content to drive the experiencer inward -- Appreciation, Gratitude, Love and Direct Cognition. The second aspect is a direct alignment with the Ascendant. This unites the conscious mind with the Infinite Source within. The third characteristic of each of the Ascension Attitudes is a mental focus on one of the root areas of the individuality that is stressed and could be more fully lived.

Understanding this description of the Ascension Attitudes is much more difficult than the practice of Ascending. Indeed, fully understanding the mechanics of Ascension is probably impossible without experiencing it.

The three-fold structure of the Ascension Attitudes causes each of the three primary aspects of our personality -- our hearts, our minds, our bodies -- to move in the direction of growth. This process unwinds or loosens the deeply held judgments and beliefs that keep us bound to fear and restriction. But this is not simply a process of introspection to remove accumulated mental, spiritual and emotional debris; this process is primarily one of effortlessly uncovering ever more expanded states of awareness.

Ascension Attitudes are called Attitudes because an attitude is a way of looking at the world. They are not called Ascension Beliefs because there is no need to believe in the Ascension Attitudes for them to work. One does not need to believe that a carrot seed planted in the ground and properly tended will grow a carrot. Belief is not required. Belief is a powerful force which can be quite useful or destructive, depending on how it is applied, but it is not required to change the nature of our lives. Carrot seeds grow carrots. The seed thoughts of the Ascension Attitudes grow a new way of looking at and living life.

Use of the Ascension Attitudes allows us effortlessly to rise beyond our previous experience of life into a state of problem-free existence. This is accomplished by aligning our limited individuality with Cosmic Universality. This underlying truth of creation can be named anything. Some call it Love. Some call it Life. Some call it the Good. Some call it Nature. Some call it Universal Mind. Some call it the Mother. Some call it Spirit. Some call it Truth. Some call it the Force. Some call it Beauty. Some call it the Higher Self. Some call it God. Some call it the Source. We call it the Ascendant. The name is supremely unimportant. What is important is to stop blocking our perception of this level of Reality.

We do not have to "open a channel" to the Source, to Universal Mind, to the Ascendant; we are all already connected. We always have been, we always will be. What *is* necessary is that we begin to remove our self-destructive beliefs and behavior patterns that are blocking this experience from our conscious awareness. Once the blocks are removed, melted, transformed, then we can make use of our birthright -- our connection to Infinite Mind. The pipeline is already there. What is necessary is to remove the self-created obstacles in the pipe that are keeping the water from flowing. It is rusty from disuse; it is blocked by the accumulated debris of life-long habits of denial and fear. But the metal is still sound; it can be cleaned relatively effortlessly and then the precious water of life will flow once more, transforming everything of our life.

The Ascension Attitudes are designed to clear out past beliefs and behavior patterns which inhibit full mental and physical functioning. By effortlessly introducing these seed thoughts at a deep and refined level of thinking, the entire structure of the mental framework gradually and gracefully transforms to reflect Reality.

Reality spelled with a capital "R" is not the reality of life mixed with suffering, the common experience of most in the world today. The capital "R" kind of Reality means that life is lived in joy, with each moment experienced fully; each opportunity is mined for its rich opportunities for progress, creativity and love. An upward spiral of consciousness is created by Ascending; a new structure of awareness is built upon the firm basis of the direct experience of Reality.

The Ascension Techniques are priceless for the modern world. The intense pace of life is simply too great to be countered without the power of a profound new Teaching. These techniques revolutionize every aspect of life by introducing new experience of inner peace, deep rest and stability.

Ascension is extremely easy to practice and quickly frees anyone from stress. This opens life to maximum creativity, enjoyment, health and success.

We all started life with innocence and brilliance. It has taken us many years to cloud our minds with self-destructive beliefs and habits. But it is easy to begin to reverse this and move back toward the freedom and power of life in the present moment. Worry and fear are not natural, they are artificially learned and maintained by our beliefs and judgments about life.

It is not hard to de-program ourselves from the hypnosis of our past and cultural conditioning. As an immediate result, life becomes easier and more enjoyable. Freedom from stress means that each moment is lived fully and completely. Every day is new with wonderful possibilities when we are no longer victimized by our past.

The Teachers of Ascension represent in this modern age an ancient teaching, founded by the Apostle John in the First Century of the Christian era. Nothing in Ascension is newly invented, every technique for stress management and meditation taught by the Teachers of The Society for Ascension has been practiced for thousands of years and has been verified to be universally true for all.

EPILOGUE: A POEM OF LIFE

In some lifetimes, I worked to create religions, philosophies, civilizations. I labored well, my products were beautiful, complex and trustworthy; my works guided and protected the lives of millions.

In other lifetimes, I realized that no organized structure, regardless how complex, true or beautiful, could ever encompass all of life. And so, seeing the obvious limits and failures of any and every organized approach to knowledge, I labored to destroy them all. This resulted often in my own demise. For example, during the Spanish Inquisition I was burned at the stake for opposing the Church. And in Peru my hands and feet were cut off for resisting the Conquistadors.

The horror of judgment and oppression is my own creation, none others. To force another to my belief was often my aim. But I have learned that forcing individuals to peace is not an answer.

An enlightened friend of mine had a vision about me in the spring of 1972 in Italy. We were driving into Roma on a fine spring day, when she suddenly turned toward me, looked at me with piercing eyes and said she had just seen me leaving behind a perfect but sterile and ruined castle in the middle of the Western Sea. She said she saw me standing alone on the shore, looking sadly back at the ruined structure. On the shore was the fecund smell of fertility; she said that the Mother of God was there, guiding me, protecting me; the redolent odor was Her scent.

I did not at the time understand her, for I felt it imperative to remain within the protecting walls of the castle of my beliefs. I was afraid that outside the castle lay chaos -- that if I were to leave the protecting turrets, battlements and colonnades of a belief system that led to the Ascendant, to God, then I would be without the Absolute, without God, hence a victim of dark and frighteningly real forces of evil, prey to the twin demons Fear and Hate. It was obvious to me that a great many, perhaps all, who did not attach themselves to a Teaching -- an organized body of knowledge and beliefs that leads to the Heart of God -- most or all of those who are not in such mighty castles are not protected from the snares and traps of the world. Those without higher aspirations of any kind often waste their lives in grotesque vices. (Which, as I recall Steinbeck observing in East of Eden, are nevertheless their best attempts to experience love.)

I felt discontented with my castle and yet berated myself for this. I felt trapped for years -- unwilling or unable to sever my connection with the magnificent teat of The Castle, afraid of the rest of the world outside its extensive and well-protected domain. Afraid of being damaged, I huddled inside its well-guarded walls.

Thinking it is possible to be damaged is a common human belief, but this does not make it true. Bodies may be damaged. Human bodies, bodies of knowledge, bodies of beliefs, bodies of organization, bodies of buildings -- all these may be hurt or fail. Yet what is failing? What is being hurt? All that is True and Real is not, can never be, hurt or even diminished in any way. Whether human minds remain constantly aware of the Truth is a different matter. But the Truth shall always remain, scintillating like a perfect jewel, beyond the confines of time and space.

After some years of this struggle, Nature conspired against me to destroy my castle. In the space of three months, my home, family, status, position and wealth were stripped from me. Lost and alone, I wandered off into the world and by great good fortune stumbled across an Ishaya, rarely travelling in the world, seeking, as it turned out, me.

My bone-chilling brush with death healed me. My terrible adversity led to glory. The wonderful Teaching of Ascension was *shared with me. A gift I could never have deserved was freely given me. Life opened where I had anticipated only the terminal ruin of degeneration and despair.*

One time when I was Ascending with the Ishayas in the Himalayas, I had a vision -- all the great and beautiful castles of the world were standing embattled and alone, surrounded everywhere by the dark and roiling sea of mindless chaos. A handful only were in the castles, working to extend knowledge of the Ascendant, to increase Truth and Beauty in the world; the rest were in the outer darkness, laboring to destroy the creations inside, some with active malicious intent, but most from apathy, ignorance, indifference.

"Why, Lord?" I thought. "Why permit this terrible war?"

At once Boanerge walked into my room, sat before me, leaned forward and tapped me gently on the chest. My mind expanded; I learned that this ancient belief of mine was cutting me off from the largest part of the Universe. All of the world's current civil wars lay in this outer chaos, for example. As did the starvation and disease in Africa. As did all the embattled and rotting cities of our civilization.

"Are all of those unfortunates then relegated to Hell?" Boanerge asked me gently. I saw his point; many fundamentalist tenets hold this to be so. If you are not a fundamentalist Christian or fundamentalist Muslim or fundamentalist New Age person or fundamentalist whatever, you are certainly going to be eternally damned. And what of those who were born before that particular religion was born? Why, they must certainly be in Hell already.

Many answer their fears by trying to build their castle walls more strongly -- they follow the dictates of the leaders of their belief system ever more exactly, delve more and more deeply into the philosophical underpinnings of the particular castle currently occupied -- but the price they pay is horrible, for surrounding their castle on every side and beating ever more forcefully on its walls are the frighteningly real and evil seas of darkness, chaos, and despair.

I saw then that my vision was distorted, for the outer form of chaos was also my creation. I created pain. I created suffering. I created war. I created starvation. I created illness. I created death. The moment I saw the perfection of the Ascendant hiding in those things that I had adjudged evil, all the castle walls on the Earth collapsed to dust and fell.

But instead of being then swamped by the Boiling Sea of Chaos, the Teachings inside the Castles expanded to encompass all of the Universe.

Said another way, I remembered then that the entire Universe was my earlier creation. And all the Castles of the Earth were as the jewels in the crown of God's perfect Love toward me, which is the same as God's perfect Love toward you and for everyone else.

Techniques that bring about Self-realization are not the same thing as Self-realization. No Castle is worth the price if it means life is divided between good and evil or between life and death. Even the magnificent perfection of the Ishayas' flawless Science of Ascension is nothing without knowing the Truth underlying it. Gathering up of techniques is the answer for no one. Only direct experience of Reality suffices to free life from death. Only full and complete enlightenment satisfies the life quest of a soul.

No man is an island, entire of itself, every man is a piece of the Continent, a part of the main; if a Clod be washed by the Sea, Europe is the less, as well as if a Promontory were, as well as if a Manor of thy friends or of thine own were. Any man's death diminishes me, because I am involved in Mankind. And therefore never send to know for whom the bell tolls. It tolls for thee.

-- *John Donne*

-- *MSI*

APPENDIX

THE SEVEN SPHERES:
THE TWENTY-SEVEN
ASCENSION TECHNIQUES

The rate of progress in Ascension is individually determined. For those moving quickly and smoothly, it is valuable to learn the sixteen techniques of the first Four Spheres in rapid sequence: every two weeks, a new technique can be acquired. And even the advanced and subtle techniques of the final three Spheres can be quickly gained for those who desire growth above all else. In the final analysis, evolution depends entirely on individual desire, how quickly one wishes to rise in the full development of consciousness.

I. ROOT STRESSES

1. PRAISE. The Praise Ascension Attitude corrects the fundamental stress of the modern world, that *something* is wrong with the individual life. This Attitude by itself is sufficient to generate full enlightenment, but because of most individuals' life-long habit of strain and divided minds, more techniques will usually be required to perfect growth. Nevertheless, the first Attitude is sufficient unto itself and will usually prove the most useful for transforming the grossest levels of beliefs and judgments about life. This Attitude above all others can be used any time of the day or night when it seems that individual life is not progressing as well as it could.

2. GRATITUDE. Similar in power for transforming the root stresses of modern life is the Gratitude Attitude. The focus here is on the objective world; this technique is designed to cure all erroneous beliefs and concepts about the body and the external Universe. It is the master key for unlocking belief in the limitations of the body, in sickness and in death; it also is the first stage in mastery of the outer world. As such, it is invaluable for healing disease of any and all kinds.

3. LOVE. For many, the Love Attitude is the sweetest of the first three; it is designed to heal all the misconceptions about our relationship with the Ascendant itself. Together, the first three techniques are capable of removing all beliefs and judgments about the limited nature of the three primary divisions of human life: subjective, objective and spiritual. These three Attitudes together are sufficient for anyone to climb to enlightenment. Further techniques are for greater acceleration.

4. COMPASSION. The Fourth Technique clarifies the relationship of the individual with all other human beings and animals. Invincibility in human life is the result of mastery of consciousness; this is based in harmlessness. (Harmlessness is called *ahimsa* in the ancient literature. Mastery of ahimsa means that no creatures ever have enmity toward you or will knowingly harm you.) Harmlessness is established by the full development of compassion, which is the automatic by-product of this technique. Universal Compassion is *the* requirement for enlightenment from the standpoint of the Ascendant. Only those who have proven they will not abuse their power are given the key to the Door of Everything.

The first four techniques are sufficient to establish Perpetual Consciousness, but the rate of growth will be slower than need be. As the body decreases in stress and the mind increases in clarity as a result of regular Ascension, the desire will naturally grow to learn ever more powerful and subtle techniques. Each Sphere of techniques is greater than the preceding: each Sphere is more subtle and more powerful than the one before. They make a spiral of increasing experience, perception and knowledge.

One function of the advanced Spheres is to develop the

subtle energy centers in the body known in the ancient literature as the chakras (literally and in the West, "wheels of fire"). The chakras are scattered like so many jewels along the spine, starting at the base and rising to the crown of the head. Development of each of these seven energy centers is required to bring about full enlightenment; Ascension provides an effortless and highly effective method for accomplishing this.

The chakras locations in the body correspond with the locations of the spine's major nerve ganglia. Among other things, the chakras control hormonal secretions, changes in circulation rate, blood pressure, respiration, blood sugar level, neuro-muscular excitation, and the endocrine glands. In the West, the memory of the chakras is retained in the image of the caduceus, the traditional symbol for the healing arts:

The open eagle wings represent fully developed consciousness, the highest degree of enlightenment, in the crown chakra. The staff represents the
sushumna, the central channel in the spine through which the energy of life rises to bring enlightenment. The two serpents represent the two subtle channels that run alongside the sushumna, the ida and the pingala. The chakras are located where the ida and the pingala cross. The ida and the pingala originate in the base of the spine

and end in the sixth chakra, in the center of the skull. The pingala is white and carries solar energy and the forces of the day. This energy moves our consciousness upward toward the rational. The ida is black and carries lunar energy and the forces of the night. Its downward movement takes us into the unconscious where we experience regeneration and intuition. In the average person, life energy flows primarily along the ida and the pingala, supplying energy to the sense organs and faculties of awareness that

maintain the illusion of the world. It is only with the awakening of enlightenment that the energy flows fully and completely up the central channel, the sushumna. When this happens, the chakras reverse their orientation from downward and outward to upward and inward.

The chakras connect our consciousness with our bodies. In the waking state, the mind experiences chaos: at least 50,000 incoherent thoughts a day race through everyone's mind, many of them mutually contradictory, many of them desiring the useless or the impossible. The physical body attempts to respond to these chaotic thought patterns; the impossibility of doing this results in sickness, failure of the organs, aging and eventually death. Most of our mental energy is literally thrown away every day in this self-destructive manner. Once the mind is freed from the source of these 50,000 thoughts -- the defenses, complexes and addictive compulsions of our habitual beliefs and judgments -- the energy of complete consciousness rises up the spine, enlivening each of the seven chakras, resulting in inner silence, perfect awareness of the Ascendant and complete and permanent bliss.

II. THE UNIVERSE

5. SOLAR. The result of the Solar Ascension Attitude is to begin to awaken the highest function of human consciousness: sahasrara, the thousand-petalled lotus of light at the top of the skull -- the seventh chakra. Maharishi Patanjali, the author of the Yoga Sutras (circa 3,000 BC), described the result of mastery of the Solar Attitude as "knowledge of the Cosmic Regions." The Cosmic Regions are the seven planes of existence or light that surround and permeate our Universe of name and form. Mastery of the Solar Technique gives complete knowledge of each of these severally and individually. It is also a powerful tool for the development of the highest degree of human enlightenment, Unity Consciousness. Mastery of the

Solar connection opens one to the Causal Worlds; upon death, this is where one goes. This is called the Path of the Sages.

6. LUNAR. The Lunar Attitude develops the intuitive power of the sixth chakra, Ajna, the "Third Eye." Patanjali describes the result of mastery of the Lunar Technique as complete knowledge of the firmament. Another result of this Attitude is the development of Soma, the glue of the Universe that is responsible for the celestial perception of the second stage of enlightenment, Exalted Consciousness. The Moon is called the "Vat of Soma" in the ancient literature, because the focus on the Moon naturally produces this molecule in the body. Mastery of the Lunar connection opens the aspirant to the worlds of the virtuous, to the Heaven of the Forefathers, to the Path of the Gods; leaving the body this way upon death takes one to the Astral Regions. This is considered a lower exit than the Solar exit, the difference corresponds to different stages of enlightenment. Those dying in Perpetual or Exalted Consciousness follow the Path of the Gods; those dying in unity attain the Path of the Sages.

7. EARTH. The Seventh Technique is designed to facilitate the movement of Awareness, so vital for the development of Unity. It is also designed to remove the last of the separation between the individual and the Universe; it is the obverse of the Love Ascension Attitude and completes it. It is a protection from all accidents. The Earth Attitude creates a refined level of witnessing, the hallmark of Perpetual Consciousness, and assists in the development of the celestial perception of Exalted Consciousness, the second stage of enlightenment.

8. PEACE. The Eighth Technique establishes Peace with all of relative creation, thereby further stabilizing harmlessness. It also has the effect of confirming the most important relationship of the individual with the Source of All that Is: the limited self surrenders to the Infinite. This Technique has the effect of stabilizing the only correct relationship with the Ascendant; this naturally results in a much faster rate of progress. It is also a key to the ability to fulfill all desires and dramatically develops celestial perception.

III. THE BODY OF THE ASCENDANT

9. BEAUTY. The Ninth Technique bequeaths the experience of the Reality of the most important aspect of the Ascendant. It also develops Soma and celestial perception. With its complete mastery, the second stage of enlightenment is permanent.

10. LIGHT. The Tenth Technique focusses on the inner petal of the sixth chakra, the petal that develops perfect intuition. Mastery of this Attitude gives complete knowledge of all that there is to be known and assures Perpetual Consciousness.

11. STRENGTH. The application of this Attitude structures the ability to heal any disease of the aspirant or of anyone else. It also develops celestial perception and Exalted Consciousness.

12. SILENCE. The Twelfth Technique stabilizes immovability of Infinite Awareness and further establishes the relationship with the Supreme quality of the Ascendant. It also has the effect of opening the first or root chakra, Muladhara, which is located at the base of the spine.

IV. THE BODY OF LOVE

13. MASTERY. The Thirteenth Technique develops perfect mastery of the body and the world. It complements the eleventh by bringing out the full ability to heal the body. Patanjali said the result of mastering this Attitude is complete knowledge of all bodily systems. This Attitude develops the third chakra, the navel chakra, Manipura.

14. POWER. The Fourteenth Technique masters desire. In its final development, it bequeaths the ability to manifest the form of all words: anything that is spoken comes to pass. This Attitude develops the fifth chakra, Visuddha, located at the base of the throat.

15. CENTER. This Attitude develops celestial perception, Exalted Consciousness, the second, outer petal of the sixth chakra, Ajna, and continual awareness of the most important aspect of the Ascendant. It also develops a refined ability to use the intellect and stabilizes the power of intuition.

16. INVINCIBILITY. The Sixteenth Technique develops the unchanging reality of perfect Love. It is the first direct application of Awareness to the all-important fourth chakra, Anahata, the heart chakra. This Technique develops the relationship with the power of the Ascendant and the full perception of the most refined qualities of the Ascendant. As such, it is a highly powerful technique for the development of the second stage of enlightenment, Exalted Consciousness.

V. GLORY

17. GLORY. The Seventeenth Attitude further refines the sixth chakra, Ajna. It develops the *Sat* (absolute) quality of the Ascendant and connects the individuality with the perfect essence of Truth. This Attitude also refines the development of the Sixth Attitude by firming the relationship with the Path of the Gods, the Lunar Path.

18. BLISS. The Eighteenth Attitude develops full use of the sushumna and further refines the seventh chakra, Sahasrara. It develops the *Ananda* (bliss) quality of the Ascendant by connecting the individual with unbounded joy. This Attitude also refines the development of the Fifth Attitude by firming the relationship with the Path of the Sages, the Solar Path.

19. LIFE. This Attitude opens the doorway to imperishable physical life. It also develops Amrita, the molecule of immortality, and the second chakra, Svadhisthana, which is associated with the sexual organs. It is the essence of mastering mastery itself, for the full development of this Attitude bequeaths the ability to transform the consciousness of others through the movement of your Unbounded Consciousness into theirs.

20. WISDOM. Mastery of this Technique results in the stabilizing of the refinement of Unity Consciousness known as all-knowingness.

VI. REVELATION

{*Note: A highly refined level of consciousness needs to be achieved before these final techniques are learned. Revelation Techniques directly reveal the underlying nature of Reality.*}

21. CONNECTION. Mastery of the First Revelation Technique gives full knowledge of the connection of the Soul to the Ascendant, the qualities of the Soul and the qualities of the Ascendant.

22. DISTINCTION. The Second Revelation Technique is designed to burn away whatever is left of the limited individuality by diving directly into the heart of the Ascendant.

23. CHARACTERISTICS. The Third Revelation Technique develops perception of the Infinite light of the Ascendant in all its varied forms.

24. FAITH. Mastery of the fourth Revelation Technique develops complete knowledge of faith and perfect one-pointedness of attention.

25. ETERNITY. The fifth Revelation Technique stabilizes the highest degree of awareness of the *Chit* (Consciousness) value of the Ascendant.

26. THE THREAD OF SOULS. The final Revelation Technique develops complete awareness of the Sutra Atman: the connecting link between all souls.

VII. BRAHMAN

27. OMNIPRESENT SPLENDOR. The final technique ties all the sundered parts of the personality together in the Ascendant to establish Unity permanently.

The Seventh Sphere also contains the Advanced Techniques for the Eighteenth and Nineteenth Attitudes. Collectively these are known as Immortality Techniques.

-- MSI

INDEX

MORE INFORMATION

For more information on the Seven Spheres, courses of instruction in the Twenty-seven Ascension Attitudes, or in-residence Ascension Teacher-training, write or call:

**SFA Publications, 23632 Highway 99 #F-196
Edmonds, WA 98026
Attn: Father Devananda Ishaya (206) 292-4970
or Sarah Cholewinski (206) 233-8433**

MSI has written a book describing his first meeting with the Ishayas called **FIRST THUNDER**. Popular author Louise Hay commented on **FIRST THUNDER**: "A wonderful book for both those beginning on their spiritual pathway and for advanced students - an enlightening story." **MSI** has also written a sequel to **FIRST THUNDER** called **SECOND THUNDER**: *Seeking the Black Ishayas* which describes his visionary experiences while studying with the Ishayas. He has also written **ENLIGHTENMENT!** *The Yoga Sutras of Patanjali, a New Translation and Commentary,* an analysis of the pre-Christian roots of Ascension. Send $12.95 for **First Thunder,** $17.95 for **Second Thunder,** or $19.95 for **Enlightenment!** plus $5 shipping and handling for each book to:

**SFA Publications, 23632 Highway 99 #F-196
Edmonds, WA 98026 Attn: Novitiate Dharani
(206) 744-8006**

ATTENTION: Quantity discounts are available on bulk purchases of **Ascension!** For information write or call:

**SFA Publications, 23632 Highway 99 #F-196
Edmonds, WA 98026 Attn: Novitiate Balarama
(206) 640-8033**